A
CANDID
CONVERSATION

LESSONS IN
LIFE, LOVE & LEADERSHIP

Published in Canada, for Global Distribution by YGTMedia Co.

www.ygtmedia.co

For more information email: publishing@ygtmedia.co

ISBN trade paperback: 978-1-998754-41-0
eBook: 978-1-998754-42-7

To order additional copies of this book:
publishing@ygtmedia.co

Author photo by Thoun"TK" Kheang

A
CANDID
CONVERSATION

LESSONS IN
LIFE, LOVE & LEADERSHIP

KATE WALKER

INTENTION

My intention for this book is that my stories, anecdotes, learnings, and insights impact, empower, or positively influence one or more readers.

My stories are personal, vulnerable, and yes, candid.

What I share in the book is based on my personal recollection and interpretation of events. Of course, recollections may vary from person to person. If someone has a different recollection, that is fair. My stories are not intended to challenge or judge anyone or anything at this time in my life.

In a way, I hope that my stories are not the plot. It's my transformation, transition, insights, new awareness, and action that are the plot.

I choose to be brave and share this book. As I get closer to publishing, sometimes I get nervous that some may judge what I share or tell me that my writing sucks. That's okay, I'm ready.

I'm ready because I will keep my focus on believing that impacting even one reader will make my decision to write and publish a book all worthwhile. That's why I'm here.

INTRODUCTION

On a spring break trip in 2022, during breakfast one morning, my sixteen-year-old son and I were discussing potential paths to abundance. This kid is a natural entrepreneur and I just love our conversations. Who resells Yeezy shoes at the age of eleven? He does.

The scenery was majestic—we were overlooking the azure Sea of Cortez. The birds chirped, the palm trees swayed, and the sun started to warm the day as we chatted about an abundant approach to supporting and serving *many* people. We talked about how books can impact hundreds, thousands, or many more at one time. Books can share helpful stories and guidance and provide value.

He then asked me if I'd thought about writing a book. I paused for a few moments and then told him that I'd actually been penning one for a few years. Here was my opportunity to practice an elevator pitch. The topic of the book was personal. Very personal. Vulnerable. How would I describe it to him?

With some trepidation, and after stumbling over the right words in my mind, I told him that my book would be a cautionary yet empowering tale for young women. It would be about self-worth, relationships, and leadership. It would explore decisions that I made due to lack of awareness and naivety.

This time my son paused. Then he said, defensively, "So, basically, you plan to trash Dad?"

"No," I said immediately. "This is a book about me."

I explained that there would be examples of some of his father's behaviors aimed at me over the years, but these would be shared with the intention of providing context. Ultimately, it would be about my experiences and how I took ownership of my choices and behaviors through a years-long journey of healing.

This book is a memoir. It reflects my present recollections of past experiences. Some of the characteristics of the people mentioned have been changed, some events have been compressed, and some dialogue has been recreated.

As I wrote this book, I gently directed myself to the idea of service. I wrote it to help people who desire empowerment. People who want to redesign their lives. I want to help readers hear the sound of the siren in their own lives.

I used to be the most hardheaded, stubborn woman on the planet. My mom tells me, with pride, "Kate, when you set your mind to something, you make it happen." I wrote this book for young women who are hardwired like me—who will see, hear, and, hopefully, be moved by my messages.

What would it have taken for me to let go of the man I was dating in my midtwenties who would later become a life partner? There were red flags all over the place. I wish I'd had resources back then—

relatable information and stories that would have helped me see and comprehend the land mines on my path.

What would it have taken for me to get a grip on my self-worth and let go of something that I thought I wanted desperately but that wasn't right for me? Honestly, someone probably would have had to kidnap and reprogram me. Better yet, what if there had been a book that had dropped into my lap to help explain some of what I was experiencing? Or a workshop that had caught my attention?

I can't go back in time, but I can now share my thoughts on the lessons learned and ultimately forgive myself for the least well-informed choices that I made on my path. I hope that this book will act as a beacon for someone out there like me.

My story is one of insecurity, trauma, desire, longing, career success, pursuit, love, marriage, kids, narcissistic personalities, gaslighting, heartbreak, intuition, strength, divorce, sadness, and reinvention. You could call it a story of rising and falling and rising again.

In this book, I share stories that might position me as a victim. What I am, though, is a survivor. Who is thriving. This is the story of my experiences, choices, and lessons. Someone once told me, "Kate, write from the scar, not the wound." Yes, there are some wounds to share, but everything led to a scar. And these scars became beautiful. The shape of them changed dramatically.

I'm compelled to write about my experiences now because I've done countless hours of personal-development work, therapy modalities, and deep reflection. The journey to self-awareness is painful, but possible. The truth hurts *and* will also set us free.

ABOUT THIS BOOK

I've titled the book A *Candid Conversation* because I'm talking about my personal journey, my vulnerable evolution, and in doing so, I'm hoping to spark conversation with and among the women who read this.

I want this book to get into the hands of women who perhaps haven't taken time to reflect on their self-worth, boundaries, and inner wounding. I want these women to find their voice and use it in a way that expresses their needs. I want these women to not silence or edit their voice to protect themselves or others. I hope that this book helps anybody who might find themselves in a situation similar to mine.

Along with my story, this book contains prompts for reflection as well as descriptions of tools that have helped me in my journey. It's unfortunate that I didn't have the tools I needed as a younger person. Now that I've grown older and wiser, I see more clearly so many relationship and self-worth pitfalls. My desire is that this book gets into the hands of the people who will find value and solace in it, and that it will help them develop sound judgment on their own paths.

Even though I *felt* fully aware and even savvy, my life often happened *to me*. Now, I guide my life, allowing it to happen *for me*.

Come along on my journey.

PART 1: LIFE

Nothing happens until you decide . . .
Make a decision,
and watch your life move forward.

– Oprah Winfrey[1]

The learning goes on and on. It's still happening, this very minute. Sometimes I wish the lessons would stop, but they keep coming. I reflect on my childhood. I reflect more deeply on it. Then, I reflect on my twenties. My thirties. My forties. I reflect more deeply. I judge myself further. I've been in deep-reflection mode for at least a decade. How can I not be fully healed—free and clear of self-judgment—after a decade of reflection? I suppose that's the human experience.

What I *can* say is that at this point in my journey, I've learned that I had no control over, or mature comprehension of, my upbringing. My mental circuitry was being hardwired based on what I saw and experienced. As a kid, you have no idea what's happening to your inner wiring. You just download, process, and move on. You don't realize you've been programmed for better or for worse—until you decide to reflect and then allow yourself to connect some dots.

Much of what happened in my childhood didn't become crystal clear until my forties and beyond. Lessons came into my mind and needed processing and then reprocessing. As children, how are we supposed to maturely or expertly process what we're seeing and experiencing? Life is just life when we're kids. Stuff happens.

How are we supposed to consciously know that the traumas experienced at school, at social events, and at the dining room table will leave an imprint on our psyches and follow us around for decades?

I will continue to grow and make better sense of my inner-child wounding and experiences. I've taken many educated guesses at my parents' childhood wounds and why they behave in certain ways. I will continue to work to drop my self-criticism and judgment while adding some sprinkles of self-compassion. After all, the experiences and the programming were normalized.

I will continue to forgive myself for the choices I've made due to my childhood norms. Finally, I will continue to work to free myself from nasty self-judgment. Self-judgment is perhaps the hardest self-defeating habit to untangle and release.

1: THE WONDER YEARS

I was born in Lowell, Massachusetts. That's where my dad grew up, but both my parents despised the frigid winters of Massachusetts and moved our family to Sacramento, California, when my brother and I were just toddlers. My dad was stationed there for a period of time when he was a captain in the US Air Force. He and my mom also wanted to put three thousand miles of distance between his family and them. Tensions were running high on that side of the family.

I grew up in a somewhat idyllic suburb. When I was five, my parents moved us into a brand-new home in a brand-new housing development. My dad was a real estate agent and sold houses in this new subdivision of Eichler-style homes. For a few years, he worked out of the neighborhood's subdivision model home and was within walking distance of work. My mom, my brother, and I would sometimes visit him at the office, which felt special.

My days were mostly spent riding my bike, going to the newly constructed, sprawling swim and tennis club, and spending carefree summer nights in our grass backyard. I was a naive and mostly happy kid. There were a lot of kids in the neighborhood, and we were all friends. We played football, baseball, and kickball, ran races, rode bikes, and were active out on the safe streets. For the most part, I was the only girl in this sporty group. I found it easy to hang with the boys. Often, I was the team captain and coordinator on the asphalt gridiron.

The vibe at school felt different. More judgmental. More serious and rigid. I wasn't the captain of the playground. Far from it. I felt meek and unseen out there. As the months and years went on, I learned something that would impact me deeply: I wasn't the popular or desired girl at school. I came to surmise that I wasn't the prettiest girl either.

At my elementary school, there was an unwritten and unspoken ranking system of desirability. I'd been assigned my rank. Nobody specifically talked about the system. There was nothing abnormal about it. There was nothing to challenge. It just was. Through this playground system, people were judged and categorized by their looks and personality. This became a learned way of life. By first grade, I already understood the concept of judge and be judged.

I came to observe that the loud, assertive kids seemed to garner attention and accolades. The loudest kids, the ones who desired the spotlight, weren't brand-new on the school scene—they'd spent their earliest years in daycare systems. I'd asked my mom to send me to daycare. My mom never sent me to daycare. Ever. I went to a cooperative preschool (parent-volunteer led) a few hours a week. A quiet kid, I didn't put myself in the spotlight. I watched and observed how things operated both verbally and nonverbally. I made note of which boys liked which girls and vice versa. I liked the boys who didn't like me back. As school life progressed, I made a few good friends. I was usually on the fringes of the popular kids but never the kid who was paid any particular attention. Not even by teachers. I blended in, faded. This felt comfortable.

The competitor in me did come out at times. I liked to win. Competition would bring out my inner fighter. I'd strive to win the book-report contests, and I even ran for student council. Deep down, I was brave when it came to competitive situations. I just didn't realize my bravery at the time. I was simply trying to achieve a win, which felt gratifying. Trying for a gold star.

It feels devastating to admit that there's a critic, a very mean judge who has lived deep within me since my days on the playground. Playground society made me believe that I wasn't the pretty, desirable, interesting girl. At a subconscious level, I internalized unworthiness. I didn't put this together until I was in my forties. As time went on in my youth, I learned to toughen up and exude confidence. This helped me feel worthy—at least at a surface level. I learned to navigate life realizing I might not be seen or heard.

Meanwhile, I was growing up in a house where my parents were increasingly drinking. My dad would take it to the point of passing out. He was usually angry, for one reason or another. Arguments happened daily, hourly. They were a way of life. I learned to shove down my feelings of fear and uncertainty. Disengaging was on my path of least resistance.

It wasn't until decades later, when I started connecting the dots, that I realized these were traumatic events. For most of my life, I believed that my childhood was a thing of the past that had zero bearing on my present. However, the events of my childhood put my mind and body in a state of hypervigilance. My need to maintain a sense of control is deep-seated in my body to this day.

Despite the drama and chaos inside the four walls of my childhood home, to the world, we conveyed the image of a perfect family. Our stuff didn't stink. We'd just put on a smile and cheery demeanor and get on with it. Putting on a cheery face and getting on with it became programming that I carried for most of my life. No matter what drama was happening at home, in public, my parents would shoot the breeze with people, exchange jokes, and relate by way of sarcasm. Smiles, everybody, smiles. I learned to act as if everything were fine.

My dad would talk crap about other people then tell my brother and me how great we were. He'd tell us that we were smarter than 99 percent of the people on the planet. I grew to generally believe my dad's words. This approach might sound like a great way to build a child's self-esteem, and perhaps he was trying to tell us that we were privileged, but his comments made my overall outlook myopic, which fostered a closed mindset. This put a filter over my self-awareness as a young person.

Our family dynamic felt normal. I never questioned my dad's view that we were awesome and everybody else sucked. Never mind my dad's nightly drinking, my mom's tears, and all of us walking on eggshells to avoid triggering any type of argument. I learned that my discomfort and normalization of bad behavior (otherwise known as dysfunction and codependency) were simply part of life.

I didn't comprehensively understand the concept of codependency until recently. It just never made sense to me. Wasn't the name of the game to support each other and have each other's backs at any cost? Nobody took ownership or accountability for their behavior. Blame was a game.

I can now see how my childhood observations and way of life shaped my overall outlook and my own behaviors.

2: QUEEN BEE

By the time I got to high school, my internal message about not being the desired one had become part of my DNA. I had accepted and come to terms with my assigned ranking. The feeling of rejection made me sad, yet it also felt normal to seem invisible to people who seemed to matter.

Of course, the person who mattered socially was the *cutest* boy. Considering someone's kindness, heart, family, values, intelligence, and hobbies—none of these things were on my radar. In the system, it was all about level of cuteness. Period. It didn't matter if that cute boy was rude to you or ignored you. Continuing to dream about him was the norm.

It didn't seem as if the smart people on campus got much positive attention. In fact, there didn't seem to be many smart people in my grade. The academic bar was low, from my perspective. Nobody talked about their academic work, especially if they were doing well. It wasn't the cool thing. Academic rigor and ambition weren't in style. It was a cultural norm. If somebody achieved something academically, my first reaction was, "How dare they," or, "How did that happen?"

For many years, I was good friends with a girl from my neighborhood who was a year older than I was. We'd play at each other's houses, go swimming at the tennis club, and go to the mall. As we became older, she became very pretty and seemingly perfect. She had silky long brown hair that was straight out of the movies. I grew to secretly admire her perfection and decided in high school that I should avoid her because she was out of my league. She went on to become her class valedictorian. I remember thinking, "What's a valedictorian? Why have I never heard of this award? How did she achieve it? Aren't people from our town stupid?" I didn't suspect her academic intelligence. She went on to UCLA. Goddess status.

Around the end of my sophomore year, I'd finally had enough of being ignored, invisible, and voiceless. Now, I was pissed off. It was time to formulate a new strategy. After so many years of fading into the background, I was feeling just plain bitchy, so I decided to cast myself in a new role: the Bitch. The girl who was mad as hell and not going to take it any longer. I didn't call her the Bitch at that time, but that was the essence of this compelling new character. If I couldn't get the guys' attention, I could turn on a fake attitude. I was going to turn the tables.

And so, I became rude toward guys—mean, sarcastic, and dismissive—pretending that I was a queen bee. My game expanded to include anyone who seemed worthy of rudeness. Not too long into playing my new role, I discovered that I was onto something. I loved being sassy and rude. It made me feel powerful. It was fun. And I started getting attention. It was working.

My personality underwent a seemingly permanent transformation. What I know *now* is that I dropped a lot of feminine energy from my personality and adopted a lot of masculine energy. As children, we yearn so deeply to fit in. How many of us alter our personalities to do so? Should we? My older, wiser self says no. Instead, we need to find the people we align with. These people might not be spending time at your usual places. You might need to look outside your immediate sphere.

One of my top values these days is kindness—giving it and spending time with people who can offer it. Later in this book, we'll explore the idea of a values audit. It's about identifying what values are most important to you, what you hold close to your heart, and choosing activities, people, and systems that support these values.

3: WINNING

Growing up, I spent time at the local swim and tennis club. When my family first joined the club, I was seven years old and would observe kids running around and having fun on the tennis courts. I wanted to be part of it, so my mom signed me up to join the clinics. I went out there with a used Jimmy Connors wood racquet with loose strings. Despite the janky racquet and my lack of skill, I had fun. I never missed a clinic and even signed up for private lessons.

Over time I got better. When I was twelve, my mom upgraded my racquet to a brand-new Chris Evert wood racquet (which lives in my garage today!). It was like a magic wand. I felt fierce. I played in the youth summer championship and ended up winning a trophy in my division. I was hooked. I wanted to play, and I wanted to win. It was the start of my career in youth tennis.

I went on to become a competitive tournament player and received a player ranking in the Northern California Tennis Association. My ranking illustrated my winning track record and prompted invitations to join higher-level tournaments. I also played varsity tennis at my high school all four years and consistently held the number-one spot. Tennis helped me build my confidence. I spent thousands of hours hitting tennis balls, usually fed to me out of my tennis coach's shopping cart.

The technical ability of my tennis strokes was probably on a professional level. My serve was a total weapon. I'm not sure if I ever clocked it, but it was fast. What I *wasn't* taught during my training days was game-play strategy—the mental aspect of the game. I got better at basic strategy through trial and error, plus years of match play.

My coach was more focused on perfecting my already perfect strokes. I could look powerful as hell hitting five hundred balls out of a shopping cart but get me into a match and I'd struggle to close it. And when I struggled, I got frustrated.

My idea of mindset work was to channel my anger and get pissed off on the court. I determined that if I got outwardly angry enough, I'd somehow win—and reveal how deeply I cared about winning. John McEnroe's temper had seemingly worked for him. The outcome wasn't quite the same for me.

A focused mindset isn't just necessary when playing a sport. It will help you in all aspects of life. You can train your mind and strengthen your mindset. It's never too early and never too late. We'll talk about mindset in more depth later in this book. For now, here are three quick tips that I've come to embrace as a wiser person: (1) if you think you can, you can, (2) keep agreements with yourself, and (3) you have to believe to achieve. These might sound cliché, but they're accessible mindset tools.

I loved it when my dad would drive me to tennis tournaments, some of which were hundreds of miles away. We'd both feel pure joy and elation when I won a match, and on our drive home, we'd celebrate with a stop at Carl's Jr., where I'd get a junior cheeseburger, fries, a Coke, and sometimes a shake. The wins were sweet.

A lost match was a "trunk slammer," a term coined by former professional player Brad Gilbert[2]—I'd throw my equipment in the trunk and my dad would slam the lid shut. We'd approach Carl's Jr. in silence and moments later it would be in the rearview mirror. No stopping after a loss. Driving past Carl's Jr. only made me more judgmental of and mean to myself. I wanted to win so badly.

My parents had one primary tip to set me up for winning: "Practice, practice, practice!" I heard that mantra over and over and over and over. And I listened. Every evening after dinner, even on freezing-cold nights, I'd head out to a court with a bucket of balls and practice my serve. Or throw balls high in the air, let them bounce, and practice my kill shot.

What I really needed to be doing was playing practice matches with other humans. I occasionally practiced with a few local tennis friends, but these usually consisted only of brief rallies, and then we'd hit the snack bar for soda and hotdogs. A couple of boys at my club were extremely good, but they didn't want to hit with a girl. There was a woman about thirty years my senior who was phenomenal, but she didn't seem to want to practice with juniors. And so the sport seemed to be one mostly of isolation and loneliness. For a few years, I had a great doubles partner, and we won a handful of tournaments. In hindsight, I should have pursued tennis as a doubles player. It was more fun.

I was seventeen years old and at the peak of my frustration because I was dedicated to practicing but not winning as much as I wanted. At this point, I felt I was missing out on the more social aspects of life because if I wasn't at school, I was usually on the tennis court. Unfortunately, my tournament rankings weren't high enough to get me a college scholarship. That was a dream that didn't come to fruition.

I quit competitive tennis at the age of eighteen, to my parents' dismay.

In hindsight, I can see that "Practice, practice, practice" was offensive to me. I *was* practicing but not yielding the results that I desired. I needed a coach who could train me on match play, and I needed mindset and mental-toughness training. I was severely lacking these skills, and a resource didn't seem to exist. Nor did my parents or I look for one. There's no way I could have succeeded at the higher level that I wanted without a different approach to my mindset and competition strategy.

In the years that followed, I devised my own mantra: "If you're not winning, you're learning."

4: FITNESS AND DISCIPLINE

At my tennis club was an incredible gym with weights, cardio equipment, and an indoor basketball court. When I got my driver's license and could drive to the club, I began working out every evening. A group of guys worked out at the same time, and eventually we started striking up conversations and forging friendships. I started gaining confidence in my ability to be sociable with the guys.

School was such a challenging social container, and I noticed that I was making better friendships outside of that environment. Outside of it, I felt I could be my sassy and playful self. To that end, I encourage anybody who's currently unable to find their social groove to look at other environments (clubs, leagues, classes, and so on). So much social warfare happens at school, but you can recover from that ridiculousness and thrive in other places.

The guys at the gym were a motley crew: a couple of wannabe bodybuilders, a wannabe Calvin Klein model, a prison guard, and a professional football player, to name a few. We'd shoot the breeze, and sometimes after our workouts, we'd hit the IHOP. The guys would carbo-load with gigantic stacks of pancakes and I'd order a Diet Coke. We had a lot of laughs and easy conversations. It was fun hanging out with these no-judgment guys—and a great opportunity to practice getting comfortable in my own skin just being myself.

One of the guys from the gym was a year ahead of me at my high school and a star athlete. He was popular, but we became friends in this non-school environment. We'd even go to dinner or to the movies. It was never romantic, just two good friends having fun. I don't think this friendship would have launched from school.

Sometimes the guys talked about steroids, and a couple of them were using them. I didn't ask questions about this, just listened. Their stories about acquiring steroids were quite interesting, as they traveled to and from Tijuana to make the purchases. Mostly, we talked about health and wellness. I soon became interested in elite fitness and began studying bodybuilding and fitness books by various women, including bodybuilder Cory Everson.

With this new interest came a strict focus on my eating habits. I'd always had a relatively healthful diet (thanks, Mom), but as my interest in health and fitness increased, I gave up beef and pork—partly for health reasons, but more so because the idea of eating an animal started grossing me out. I'd driven the I-5 in California numerous times between Sacramento and Southern California and couldn't help noticing the cattle farms and thinking about how cows were, in fact, where hamburgers and steak came from. When I was a kid, practically every meal I ate had meat in it. The more I thought about it, the more the idea of eating cows and pigs turned me off. I haven't had beef or pork since my twenties. I haven't missed the flavor nor the heavy feeling in my stomach afterward.

As I experimented with elite fitness, I also gave up tortilla chips and similar processed items. No more chips and salsa. And no sugar treats. During this time, I was very strict and would beat myself up for making an occasional poor food choice.

These days, "forbidden" food items are back in my repertoire, but in moderation. Moderation is something I've come to appreciate. Really, it's all about how you feel. Do you gauge how you feel after eating various snacks or meals? If you're interested in wellness, you may want to experiment with different foods as well as different forms of movement to determine how they make you feel. Lately, I've noticed that eating sugary treats at night makes me feel icky in the morning. It's a harsh reality because I enjoy these treats, but my body is starting to tell me no.

For me, though, moderation has become more important when it comes to alcohol.

5: PARTY'S OVER

My thoughts on alcohol consumption have evolved and changed over the years. And they're still evolving and changing. Alcohol is a massive part of our society and culture. Having a drink in hand can help us feel more comfortable and as if we're having more fun.

When I was growing up, it was normal for me to watch my parents drink. Nothing seemed unusual about their daily ritual. Come 5:00 p.m., it was drinking time—ice cubes clinked in the cocktail glasses, beer cans cracked open, and liquor poured out of bottles with a *gulp-gulp* sound.

My dad would sit on the couch in a spot that allowed for excellent viewing of the TV. He was a sports enthusiast, and there was usually a baseball, football, or basketball game playing, New England teams preferred. He'd also watch the nightly news. Growing up in the seventies, I recall the terror of listening to the broadcasts warning us of impending nuclear war and the gasoline crisis. I guess the news hasn't changed much over the decades.

Options were aplenty in the liquor cabinet, and a variety of drinks could be poured depending on my parents' moods or the moods of their guests: vodka and grapefruit soda, scotch and soda, scotch and water, gin and tonic, vermouth, boxed wine, and a variety of beer.

Sometimes I'd open the liquor cabinet and peer at the bottles and labels. I'd reach in and grab a bottle to hold and look at. I might even open it and smell the alcohol. Each type had a distinctive scent. I don't recall my parents specifically telling me that alcohol was only for adults, but I got that feeling, and I wasn't interested in trying it as a kid.

I remember the liquor store my dad always went to. I liked going with him because he'd buy me gum or a candy bar. Our cart likely contained scotch, beer, and a Twix bar. These outings were positive bonding experiences with my dad.

My dad drank, quite possibly, thousands of cans of a particular brand of beer over his drinking career. The sight of the cans is still imprinted in my brain. They'd be strewn all over our garage and even the backyard. My brother and I would crush them before taking them to the recycling center to earn a few dollars. The beer left in the cans would splash on our shoes, and I didn't like the smell, especially on a hot day. Nonetheless, we did what it took to make our money.

Over the years, I felt a change in the household dynamic. Drinking stopped being a fun, spirited kind of activity and became something more troublesome. I started to witness its effects more keenly. As my parents fought more and more, I became angry—at alcohol. I could see that during the day, my parents were reasonable people. Conversations were calm. I liked this state of being very much. But once they started drinking, the mood changed. Tempers changed.

Who's coming out tonight? I'd wonder. *Sloppy drunks? Slurring drunks? Easygoing drunks? Will they fall asleep while sitting up?* I never knew.

At times I'd join in the yelling in an attempt to get my parents to stop their yelling, and I'd also take it upon myself to pour the big bottles of hard liquor down the sink. *If the booze isn't there, maybe they'll stop drinking,* I reasoned. Replacement bottles would quickly appear. My interventions didn't work.

My parents' constant fights became normal, though unsettling. It seemed there was always something to argue about. If my dad wasn't yelling at my mom, my brother or I would become the target. He liked to point out our deficiencies. Particularly, he told us that we were lazy. He'd yell about how I wasn't practicing tennis enough. Or winning the big matches. Whatever. Over time, I learned to disengage and walk away. There was no use in trying to have a civil dialogue; no one would win against him.

You've probably heard the old saying "Don't cry over spilled milk." Well, spilling milk—or *anything*, for that matter—would lead to upset in our home. Tensions increased when the sun went down. In the dinnertime hours, I'd pray for a functional garbage disposal. That garbage disposal was the bane of our existence. It was always breaking down. We all learned a very important lesson: Do not, I repeat, *do not* put potato peels down the garbage disposal. At one point I figured we should just stop purchasing potatoes altogether.

Why can't Mom and Dad just buy a new garbage disposal and save themselves countless DIY-plumbing nightmares and yelling? I'd contemplate solutions. As a child, I thought that the matter of the garbage disposal was hugely important, significant, and that the arguments about it were critical. These arguments could ruin an entire night, or even a week.

Of course, I eventually learned that rarely were the fights about the object itself. I can now safely assume that my dad was angry about something else and, deep down, it wasn't about the spilled milk or the broken garbage disposal.

***

One night when my parents were especially angry with each other, my brother and I were watching TV in our family room. When he and I were much younger and the booze didn't flow so heavily, we'd have dance parties with our parents in the middle of the floor on the rectangular Oriental rug. My dad would turn on his Beatles records and we'd dance and laugh. Sometimes we'd play some John Denver too. Those family nights were precious and joyful.

On this night, the dance floor became something different. My mom came flying into the room with my dad close behind her. The two of them were no more than four feet away from my brother and me as we sat on the couch, and their positions made them look as if they were in a boxing ring, which in a sense they were. It was the first time I saw them get into a physical altercation. Thankfully, they soon calmed down. These things get imprinted in your memory, but your mind does its best to suppress them.

Afterward, my mom retreated to her bedroom. Once some time had passed, my brother and I went in to quietly check on her. In her usual fashion, she tried to console us through her tears, to assure us that everything was okay. My dad just sat silently in the family room and watched TV.

That night was never discussed again. Not by any of us. I was learning a life lesson: one should dismiss things that are upsetting and even inappropriate. Smile through the tears.

I know now that there are behaviors that are never okay. If you need help making sense of behaviors aimed at you, seek professional help. Not only is it good to share your truths—you might also uncover new ways to thrive.

***

Sometimes my parents would host dinner parties. I always felt the specialness in the air during the preparation for these events. My mom was a very good cook and would put together gourmet hors d'oeuvres and multicourse meals. She'd also take the booze out of the liquor cabinet and set up a beautiful bar area where people could mix and refill their own drinks. I found her little bar area quite fabulous. Sometimes I'd ask if I could pour myself club soda or ginger ale on the rocks in her bar area—it felt very grown up.

On the mornings after the parties, the house would be littered with empty glasses, empty plates, and overfilled ashtrays. I'd try to clean things up. After all, I wanted an unobstructed view of the TV and a clean area to watch my morning cartoons.

I remember one postparty morning well. I woke up to find the house immaculately clean. Not a single dirty glass in sight. What really caught my attention, though, was the empty dining table. My mom would usually leave a tablecloth, her floral centerpiece, and candles on the table. That morning, my mom was unusually quiet and seemed angry. When I asked her what was going on, she said that my dad had gotten sick the night before. The table had been cleared, the house cleaned, and the party abruptly disbanded.

I came to find out that my dad threw up on the table surrounded by party guests. The parties stopped after that.

***

My family wouldn't just host parties. We also attended an annual Christmas Eve gathering at the house of a couple my parents knew. This couple didn't have children for us to play with, but they still made my brother and me feel included in the festivities. For us, that meant being served unlimited soda—something that was forbidden at our house. The adults would imbibe alcohol and get merry.

One year, the party went very late. My brother and I fell asleep, and when my parents were ready to go, they woke us up and carried us to the car. My stomach quickly tied itself into knots when I realized that my dad was drunk at the wheel. I woke right up, and my backbone was as straight as a rod as I sat in the middle of the backseat. I needed to have the best view of the steering wheel and the road. I became hypervigilant, watching and anticipating. I prayed that he'd steer properly and get us home safely. My mom sat there in silence. I assumed she was intoxicated too and had deferred the driving to him.

It was a memorable thirty minutes of my life. After all, praying to God that your car doesn't swerve off the road, swerve into another car, or hit another car head-on takes deep concentration.

I'm so grateful for the initiative of Mothers Against Drunk Driving and their hard work that changed laws and cultural norms around drinking and driving. The concept of a designated driver is truly a lifesaver.

If you think your kids aren't watching, listening, and being impacted by your behavior, you're incorrect. Even if your drinking is social, children are still watching. As adults, we get to make our own decisions and run our own lives. Nobody likes being told what to do. But if alcohol consumption is a part of your home or social life, it could be worth doing an audit of how it might be affecting you and your family. Is it hindering the peace and stability of your home?

***

In my junior year of high school, I was categorically angry. My parents had started calling me out on my bad attitude. Yes. I had a bad attitude. I couldn't make sense of my experience at the time, but I was certainly being impacted by my home environment.

It got to the point where I was so angry with my dad and about how he treated me (and my mom and brother) that I stopped talking to him. Trying to have any type of rational dialogue with him felt pointless. I went silent and refused to engage with him. During these years, I learned that silence could be used as a weapon.

My parents thought my behavior was simple teenage angst, but that was only part of it. Living in a constant state of uncertainty and walking on eggshells inside of my own home was too much for my nervous system. I couldn't comprehend it, but my system was building coping mechanisms. Operating with anger was one of them.

Unfortunately, the relationship between my dad and me deteriorated for many years. Time and space were needed. We began to rebuild our relationship when I had kids. We all call him Grandpa—his own reinvention.

For years into adulthood, I assumed that my childhood dynamics were in the rearview mirror—that they were simply past experiences that had no impact on my present day. Not so fast! The programming was lodged deep in my subconscious. It wasn't until I was in my forties that I sat down with myself to think about what had transpired and how it had impacted me.

It made me angry that my parents' drinking disrupted the household, but I believed it was ultimately *their problem*, not mine. I believed that once I graduated from high school, this alcohol business, the fighting and household chaos, would become a distant memory. My physical exit from my childhood home would surely resolve the issue.

Today, I give kudos to my dad for choosing to become sober around the time I headed to college. I've never talked to him in depth about this decision, but over the years he's made a few pointed comments about his choice. Namely, about how consuming alcohol has no good purpose. About how it ages people physically and mentally. He's proud of his decision and commitment and is thirty-five years sober at this point. He quit cold turkey and didn't look back.

I share more about my own experience with alcohol consumption later in the book. A question I often ask myself now is this: "What do I want my present-day relationship with alcohol to be like?" Many experiences and periods of reflection have led me to this question. I continue to contemplate the answer.

6: SMOKE AND MIRRORS

My mom continued drinking after my dad stopped. I believe that she thought she wasn't the one with the problem, that she considered herself an occasional social drinker. Her husband was the one with the problem, and she could continue "enjoying" a glass of wine or a cocktail. She tended to drink alone, away from my dad. For many years, her drinking didn't faze me or make me ponder anything.

My mom was also a smoker. During my youth, she smoked about a pack a day. She'd even smoke in the bathroom while doing her hair and makeup in the morning. I'd be fast asleep only to be woken by secondhand smoke wafting into my room and my lungs. It bothered me, but what was a girl to do? It was just what my mom did, and I had to deal with it.

She'd drive my brother and me around while smoking with the windows rolled up in her station wagon. I smelled like cigarette smoke and didn't even know it until I was in my teens, when my friends told me. Once I was made aware of this, I became embarrassed and ashamed. How can you not know that you reek of smoke? I couldn't smell my smoke-infused clothes. The total lack of awareness was a lot to wrap my mind around.

In high school, many people in my circle tried cigarettes. Clove cigarettes were popular, and I loved the smell of them, but the story was that cloves "burned your lungs." The thought of that was enough to make me say no.

My firsthand and secondhand exposure to cigarettes in my childhood made me abhor the idea of smoking. I had zero interest. I've never smoked—except for one cigarette on my alcohol-laden twenty-first birthday.

My mom started trying to quit when I went away to college. She even got the house painted and bought new couches in what I saw as an attempt to encourage a smoke-free house. When I was home for a visit in my twenties, I looked for my mom only to find her having a cigarette outside, at the side of the house. It was somewhat comical to see her sneaking around like a rebel kid. She was trying as hard as she could and knew it was important for her health to quit. Today, I'm proud of her for finally kicking her four-decade habit.

As I got older and began to reflect more on the difficult days in my family home, my mom's drinking finally started to bother me. She'd crack open a bottle of wine before dinner and offer me a glass. For years, I simply said, "No, thank you." My reason for saying no was twofold. First, the thought of drinking alcohol in that house just felt strange and wrong. Second, I wanted to support my dad in his sobriety. Why would we drink in front of someone who was sober? Why would we taunt and tease our history?

Eventually, I got curious and began asking her questions about her drinking. She didn't want to hear them. They made her defensive. As she continued to drink, my awareness grew more acute. I could see her personality undergo a transformation when she drank. She slurred her words. She became self-righteous and smug. I didn't like this personality. I liked my normal mom.

If something set her off when she was tipsy or drunk, she'd walk away. Then came the silent treatment. Her silence would trigger me. Getting iced by my mom was the worst. When would we get back to normal? When would the ice thaw? When would she make eye contact with me? When would she offer a few words?

In the words of holistic psychologist Nicole LePera, "The silent treatment is so traumatic for a child because it's not only a form of emotional neglect, it's a targeted message: 'When you upset me, you no longer exist.'" She goes on to say, "Done over and over, this creates a deep abandonment wound."[3]

It was only recently that I finally let my thoughts fly—at a family dinner. My mom asked the group, "Who would care for a glass of wine?"

What kind of fake show was this? I was done withholding my thoughts. "I don't want a glass of wine!" I blurted. "Let's admit that alcohol is a problem in this family. It was destructive in my childhood, it was destructive in my marriage, and I'm not interested in drinking alcohol."

My statement was followed by momentary silence. The only person my message seemed to register with was my younger son. Everybody else gave me the side-eye and then moved the conversation along.

I've had many conversations with my kids about alcohol, and I've held nothing back about my history and my feelings on the topic. When they were very young and I was still married but knee-deep in difficulty, I'd echo my dad's sentiment, telling my kids that alcohol serves no good purpose, really. Since then, I've shared this opinion regularly with them. I want to be honest about the impact alcohol had on me and our family.

If others' behaviors have come to bother you, you have the right to speak up. You have the right to make a different choice. You have the right to take a different point of view about something you used to ignore. You have the right to reflect on old patterns that no longer serve you. Life evolves, as it should.

I'm not sharing these stories to embarrass or shame my parents. They were doing the best they could with the tools and resources they had when I was growing up, and presumably with their own childhood wounding. I share these stories because these experiences impacted me and I was unable to realize it until my forties. I hope that I can offer a different perspective to someone reading this.

I felt safe as a very young child. I was desperate to feel that safety again as my household changed in my adolescence, and I can see now why I became so angry. I just wanted safety and normalcy.

The more I reflect on my childhood and marital homes, the more I realize that both broke down due to substance abuse. Do we really need to bring substances, even "socially," into our homes when we're raising children? How clear and lucid are we when imbibing? I haven't been perfect, but I am deeply contemplating these questions.

I encourage you to approach them with curiosity. Without judgment.

7: NOT THAT INNOCENT

In my junior and senior years of high school, the popular kids hosted and attended keggers. I thought beer tasted disgusting, but to look cool, you needed to at least hold a cup. Wine coolers eventually made their way onto the scene. Although these sweeter beverages weren't as yummy as soda, I drank them, as they were easier to consume than beer.

In high school, I got buzzed a couple of times. It was kind of fun. Funny. Entertaining. Stupid. A different kind of freedom. But I didn't get hooked on the feeling. I drank only as required to fit in.

San Diego State University was deemed a party college when I attended it, and it lived up to its reputation. I took my education seriously, but Thursday through Saturday nights, I was ready and eager for the good times. Keggers were readily available for the under-twenty-one crowd, and the name of the game was to pursue intoxication. Getting drunk was the goal. Being carefree and slightly obnoxious was the fun and desired outcome.

Dare I talk about the fun times in Tijuana, Mexico, where the legal drinking age was eighteen?

Things only got more fun in college when I turned twenty-one and could legally go out drinking with friends. The over-twenty-one crowd was at the trendy bars and clubs, and my crew would head down to Pacific Beach and the surrounding area to party. Thankfully, designated drivers were, in fact, designated before a night out. We always had a safe plan.

During these years, my reflections about alcohol were limited to how overuse made me feel. It didn't feel good to get too drunk and therefore get too hungover. As I learned more about my body's chemistry and tolerance, I embraced the concept of *it feels good to feel good.* I dialed back just a bit. I liked to be in control.

In no way was I reflecting on how alcohol had affected me and my family in the past and how I wanted to process that. Not on my radar one bit. The past was the past, with zero impact on or relevance to my present.

After college, I continued to drink socially. At business events, I'd pace my intake. If I was with friends, I'd take a more carefree approach to my drinking. When my ex, Tom, and I began getting to know each other, alcohol was a big part of our equation.

In the early days of our relationship, I wanted to be funny, cool, and likable. I'd try to match him, beer for beer. I drank a lot of beer in those days. When he flew into LA, where I lived, I'd pick him up at the airport after work with an ice-cold twelve-pack stashed in my trunk. We'd kick off the night by heading to a bar or to dinner, where one beer after another would be ordered.

We were laying a foundation for our relationship—one in which excessive alcohol was normal.

What I really enjoyed were our day trips to Napa Valley. I'd never drank wine up until that point. At least not the finer labels. The Napa experience felt sophisticated and regal. I loved that feeling. It was a pivotal time for me. I felt as if I were graduating from college days, keggers, and canned beer. Napa involved tasting wines, noshing on cheeses, and dressing up to look the part. It was our Napa dates that made me start believing I was with a sophisticated partner.

If we were out for dinner, alcohol was a certainty. Rarely were we out and not drinking. I didn't need alcohol—I never felt addicted. It was fun and a way to feel included. It was more of a habit than anything.

Over the years, I dialed back my drinking again because I didn't like the way it made me feel. I disliked when my head felt slow and cobwebby. My body felt puffy and bloated. I'd also reached a point where partaking in drink after drink was exhausting. In some circles, being hungover was a victory—something to be proud of. A hangover meant you'd got after it the night before. At times, drinking felt less like a leisurely, enjoyable pursuit and more like a game to see who could drink the most. I was fine to lose this game.

During one Christmas season, Tom and I were out and about attending various holiday events. The drinking and partying went on and on, day after day. I was drinking a lot. On New Year's Day, at the local bar for a football game, I intentionally didn't order anything because I felt gross and exhausted. But one of our friends proceeded to order me a vodka, and then there I was. Drink in hand: check. I couldn't believe I was continuing with this marathon.

That holiday season was a turning point in my relationship with alcohol. Enough was enough. I'd had it with the volume I was consuming.

I was tired of it being a priority, and the significant focus on going out drinking in pursuit of intoxication no longer resonated with me.

Former president George W. Bush quit drinking immediately after his fortieth birthday, and I remember being intrigued by what he said about it: "I don't need this in my life. It's robbing me of my energy. It's taking too much of my time."[4]

This totally made sense to me. I could relate.

When I got pregnant, I stopped drinking entirely except for a glass of wine at a couple of fancy dinners. And when I was raising my children, I rarely had a drink. My best friend also significantly reduced her alcohol consumption when her kids were very young. She said something that stuck with me: "If I was buzzed or drunk and something happened to my kids, I could never forgive myself." I hadn't thought about it this way before. My husband continued drinking, so I was happy to be the sober parent.

Again, I'm not perfect. I'm not telling anybody what to do. I'm sharing these stories and my experiences to serve as starting points for reflection.

8: FINAL DAYS OF HIGH SCHOOL

I've shared a lot about not being the "chosen" one in high school. That identity felt true for me. Despite this, I was always trying to look and feel cute in my own way. In my senior year, I began growing out my hair. I'd reached a height of five foot ten, and my body was thin and athletic. I was also starting to look like a young woman. Some of the boys were beginning to talk to me, but I was too naive to make anything of this. I thought it was a result of my trying to be less shy.

My two best friends at the time began talking about how they were gaining weight; meanwhile, I wasn't dieting. They started calling me a bimbo. I can only guess that I'd become a threat in their eyes. And as the final days of high school ticked away, these friends, whom I'd been close with since first grade, turned against me. I was already on the social fringes, and they decided to push me further away from fitting in by pulling abusive stunts. They'd ignore me, laugh at me in front of people, and exclude me from the lunch table, along with other bully antics. Meanwhile, I kept working to quietly integrate. I'd roll with the punches and just hang in there, hoping that this behavior toward me would end.

One sunny spring day after school while I was sitting in the bleachers with a large group, one of my so-called friends grabbed me by the shoulders and pinned me down while the other friend broke out a can of whipped cream and sprayed it all over my hair, face, and clothing. To say I was shocked was an understatement. All the bystanders, including classmates that I'd known for years, laughed in delight.

Shaken and embarrassed, I left the stadium in tears, my eyes barely able to focus due to the oils from the whipped cream. I was mortified. Did I tell *anyone*? No.

I was being physically assaulted by my best friends, but I didn't call it assault at the time. I called it "friends being mean." Of course, hindsight is 20/20. I should have reported my friends to the principal. Their parents should have been notified. They should have been suspended for this abuse. I said nothing.

Trying to move on and keep my chin up, I decided to team up with one of these friends to go on a double date for the prom. After all, she was my *best* friend, right? I was loyal. We asked boys we knew from another high school—it was cutting edge to bring a date from the outside, not to mention the selection of cute and available guys at our high school was limited. The dance itself was pleasant, and then everybody moved to an after-party at someone's house.

It was around 11:00 p.m. when the next round of hazing began. My other "best friend" confronted me on the back porch.

"Do you know that you're a fucking bitch?" she said. "I want to punch you out."

"Yeah!" said my double-date bestie, smirking and slurring her words. "Do it, dude!"

My friend's fist landed on my right eye socket. Again, I was shocked. My instinct was to punch her back, and we got into a little altercation before others broke it up. Here I was, with a best friend from first grade physically assaulting me while my other best friend egged her on. This abuse led to a black eye and a bruised ego.

What did I do? I tried to shrug it off and carry on. I went home that night holding back tears and wondering what the hell was happening.

My loyalties ran so deep. It took me years to realize that loyalty doesn't mean putting up with abusive behavior. People will show you who they are. I implore you to believe them. I wish somebody had taught me this when I was a teenager.

The next morning, my mom and I drove to San Diego early in the morning so that I could participate in a freshman college orientation. We drove for hours on the long stretch of Interstate 5 in central California, with its desolate early-summer fields and brown rolling hills as far as the eyes could see. Bleak scenery. My eye hurt. I felt like crying again but held back my tears and put on a cheerful face for my mom. After all, she'd taught me to be always cheerful. Put on the game face. Which I did. I'd put makeup on the bruise and kept my sunglasses on. I didn't tell her about the events of the previous evening.

As I reflected during that drive, I was hard on myself. *What could I have done to deserve that? How can I get the friendship back to how it used to be?*

Interestingly, nobody who'd witnessed what had happened reached out to offer support or ask if I was okay. The abuse had been observed and normalized. I didn't contemplate the unacceptable wrongs and how I might report them and bring justice to the situation. I didn't even know that was a possibility. I felt that accepting the abuse, being upset, and then moving on was the most normal thing I could do.

Don't put up with this kind of behavior, no matter your age. Report it. Find helpful advocates. Seek professional help. These behaviors aren't normal. You aren't "crazy."

A few weeks later, I was at the house of the friend who'd egged on the punch. (Yep, I just kept going back.) She and her mom greeted me outside, and her mom had a huge smile on her face. "Hi, Kate," she said with a chuckle. "I heard you got initiated with whipped cream at the stadium!"

I was both angry and embarrassed that this antic had been shared and was being considered humorous. *I guess it's funny to get "hazed"?* I didn't know what to say, so my eighteen-year-old self didn't reply and buried the comment.

I didn't have the wisdom or words back then to speak up and advocate for myself. But you can learn to speak up for yourself at any age. Don't delay.

9: CHANGE IS IN THE AIR

During my junior year of high school, before the bullying incidents, I attended College Night at another high school. College Night was a pivotal life event for me. My dad had gone to Boston College but didn't talk a lot about it, apart from mentioning he'd been awarded a scholarship that helped him fund his schooling. Despite the fact that he'd been to college, we didn't talk much about my college aspirations or what I might want in the future.

College Night opened my eyes to colleges that I'd never heard of, in places that I'd never dreamed of. That night, I listened to speeches about the benefits of going to college and the different academic paths available, and these messages got my attention. I'd never been part of a conversation about what the future could hold if you attended college. I felt as if I'd been invited into an exclusive room. My adrenaline was pumping. I was onto something exciting. From that day forward, college was on my radar, and I was one-hundred-percent ready for it. I was on a mission.

I knew that college would be a great path out of my hometown and the limited box of schoolyard society. I could feel that something different was possible for me. The beautiful college brochures gave me permission to intentionally consider a new way of doing life.

My childhood school environment didn't nurture me academically. My grades in high school were okay but not stellar. Often the course material and the way it was taught didn't click for me. Math, chemistry, and biology didn't excite me. The concepts I learned in these classes didn't stick in my brain, and the teachers didn't help me relate the technical concepts to real life. How would I ever use these math equations in the real world? My homework and study efforts were admirable, though. I tried. I cried.

I was mediocre at taking tests, and my grades reflected that. I had no strategy for test-taking. I learned later in life that you can be trained to take tests well. It's a shame that I wasn't taught preparatory tools or skills. It simply wasn't the culture of the school or community.

Writing assignments were a different story. I enjoyed writing because it didn't involve memorizing confusing concepts. You could just ... write.

With my modest GPA, I applied to two colleges—San Diego State University and California State University, Long Beach. My dream school, Pepperdine, wasn't feasible, both in terms of my academics and my finances, but I hoped that the colleges in Southern California would be my ticket to personal freedom and reinvention.

I'll never forget the day that I got home from high school and saw an envelope addressed to me from SDSU. I opened it immediately. The moment I read *You've been accepted*, it seemed as if the heavens opened for me. I felt an energetic zing throughout my body. It was all happening. I pumped my fist and said a quiet but powerful "YES!" My life was unfolding with possibilities, and my gut told me that there was a brighter future ahead for me. This felt like a life-changing moment. It was.

My decision was made. I'd be heading to sunny San Diego for college.

In my senior year of high school, I was feeling drawn toward a career in journalism and communication. I had a New York City poster in my bedroom, and I dreamed of working there. I started envisioning myself co-anchoring *The Today Show*, and a few classmates wrote in my high school yearbook that they hoped to see me there someday. I'd tell people that they could expect to see me taking over Jane Pauley's seat (it's Savannah and Hoda in the seat these days). Thinking big made me feel hopeful.

Know that you don't have to be a victim of the academic system in which you were brought up. There are greener pastures. Embrace the possibility of a different, better situation. Despite what your grades might tell you or how your teachers interact with you, trust that positive outcomes are possible. Being open to hearing and learning about new avenues can help you chart a fulfilling course. Keep your eyes and ears open.

I was one of the first to arrive at Zura Hall at SDSU for move-in. Feeling upbeat and confident, I was ready for my next chapter and my reinvention. After my mom moved me into the dorm, it was time for her to go. We parted ways, both of us with tears in our eyes. The drop-off was emotional, but I couldn't have been more excited to get my new life started.

SDSU was buzzing with electricity. I mean, major electricity. It buzzed through my body. The dorm, the campus, the people—everything felt incredible. I was walking on air and felt a different confidence brewing.

Southern California was magical. A world away from Sacramento. I'd come to the right place.

But the unspoken messages and subliminal feedback of my youth continued at the many fraternity parties. I wasn't the prettiest one nor the desired one. There were tons of beautiful girls who were sexy, flirtatious, loose, and free. Meanwhile, my vibe was casual, athletic, sporty.

At parties, I felt the need to bring back my high school persona, the Bitch, to make things more enjoyable for myself. I'd give the cute guys dirty looks and drop mean sound bites. It was a strategy that gave me confidence. Still, the guys were looking for the hot girls, not the mediocre-looking girls, even if they had fun personalities. The fun and friendly girls were buddies but not dating or girlfriend material.

I hadn't eliminated all my limiting beliefs, as I hadn't been given the tools yet. But attending college away from home helped me realize that I could become an even more authentic version of myself.

New beginnings are beautiful. Reinvention is beautiful. Anything is possible. You don't have to carry a heavy knapsack of limiting beliefs or preappointed identities as you evolve to your next chapter. Don't let your current circumstances dictate your future. New possibilities await you if you can dream them up and put a plan in motion. Sometimes it's simply a matter of putting yourself in a new environment and interacting with a few new people. Small changes can positively influence your path and your outcomes.

10: WORKING GIRL

In my early twenties, when I was just launching my career, wealth consciousness wasn't on my radar. Money: Others had it. I didn't. Abundance seemed elusive.

I believed that earning a good living would take decades and involve a slow climb up a steep corporate ladder. Career success was a distant goal that I'd have to work hard for. I never considered how much money I *wanted* to earn. Did I have a say in the matter? Receiving enough to pay my bills seemed reasonable.

My money story was that you made money by paying your dues and biding your time—I didn't know of any other way. I enthusiastically and willingly signed up for the nine-to-five corporate structure. I had limiting beliefs and a lack of knowledge about what else might be possible.

As young people, how are we supposed to know what we don't know? How was I to know at the age of twenty-two that I could work or earn in ways that were outside of standard systems and norms? I was living a subconscious program: pay your dues and hustle and grind for payment.

I maintained my enthusiasm for health and fitness throughout college. I joined local gyms, ran around the track with friends, and took swim and tennis classes on campus. In my junior year of college, I decided to apply for a job at a health and fitness club. I figured it was a great idea—I loved to work out, and I could help others do so and get paid for it.

I was hired as a trainer at a club that offered numerous fitness classes, and my role involved teaching aerobics classes. I'd never taught one, although I had taken many. My boss was a petite, spunky woman who taught the group of trainers. She taught us two different routines. Once we'd learned the routine and could teach it, we'd receive our class schedules. As a newbie, I had to teach the 6:00 a.m. class twice a week. Early mornings aren't my favorite time of day, and mustering up the energy to teach at that hour wasn't easy.

The 6:00 a.m. classes were packed. I'd walk in wearing my leggings and tightly cinched T-shirt—part of our mandatory uniform. Then I'd put on the cassette tape of my choosing, grab my handheld microphone with the very long cord (no cordless mics back then), and get up on the carpeted riser so that everybody could see and follow the aerobics routine. I felt like a spectacle. Nonetheless, I'd bring my high energy and move to the beat of Wham! and other bands of the nineties.

One morning I was a bit hungover and had to extract myself from bed when the alarm went off. I drove to work that morning feeling bitter, and when I arrived, I was tired and loopy. I hit play on the stereo, got up on the riser, and looked around the room. Once again, it was packed. Then, as the class got going, I started laughing—I got a case of the giggles and couldn't stop myself. Soon, others were cracking smiles and giggling with me. It was 6:00 a.m., and I just wanted to be back in bed, not faking perkiness in this dark, early morning hour! I was over it. *What am I doing here?* After that class, I knew I needed to request a new schedule.

I set up a time to talk with my boss. At this point, I'd been employed for three months and was in the swing of things. Not only was I going to ask her for a schedule adjustment—I was also going to ask for a raise. I'd been doing well, and my minimum-wage earnings seemed meager for the physical effort that I'd been putting in.

We sat down and talked about my schedule first. Next, I broached the topic of money. I gave her a couple of performance-based reasons why I wanted a raise and then told her about my friend who worked at a deli café and made two dollars more per hour than I did. I talked about her role at the deli and explained that I provided more results in my job.

Once I finished my speech, my boss leaned in and said, "Let me ask you something." She paused for several moments. "Would you rather have a great day of physical fitness and smell like sweat when you walk out of here? Or would you rather walk out of your job smelling like PICKLES?"

My eyes grew wide. She had me stumped. I was speechless. Of course I didn't want to smell like pickles. I didn't have a comeback. So, she won that argument. No raise, and my schedule barely changed.

I ended up quitting a few months later. I couldn't get over the feeling that my efforts were too much of a grind. My boss's refusal to have a serious conversation with me was disappointing. The pickle defense is one that I won't forget.

As life progresses, we learn more about what we want—and what we don't want. About what feels good and what doesn't feel good. You might find yourself in a role where you're viewed not as a valuable contributor but as an unappreciated employee who keeps the factory running. It's okay to make a change. I'd thought that I wanted to work out and get paid for it, but the early morning shifts weren't for me. Listen to your body and your mind. Ask for what you want. I wasn't lazy for not wanting to work at 6:00 a.m. It simply wasn't my preference, and that preference couldn't be accommodated.

I also realized that I wanted to work somewhere that offered a more distinct career ladder, so I aimed my compass in that direction.

***

After I earned my BA in speech communications from SDSU, my first corporate job was in Beverly Hills. At twenty-two years old, I started working in the music division of a major talent agency as an agent assistant—specifically, for the agent of a music megastar.

I was acquaintances with a professional model who traveled between Los Angeles and New York, and she was willing to let me sublet her LA apartment during my transition from San Diego. Not too long after I moved, the Northridge earthquake occurred. The 6.7 magnitude quake gave me a ride I'll never forget. California living at its scariest.

While I was out hustling in my new, time-consuming job, she was receiving messages on her answering machine about yoga classes in New York. *Wow*, I thought. *What a lifestyle! How lucky to be a gorgeous model who takes yoga classes during the workday.* In my limited mind, that kind of expansive lifestyle was accessible only to the beautiful and wealthy.

I felt as though I were on a normal path, paying my dues and hustling. At the time, this felt good to me. Myth alert! Paying your dues in a systemic structure is *optional*. There are other paths that can potentially take you where you want to go.

At the agency, the talent division was much more prestigious than the music division, or so it seemed. The building I worked in housed the music division and the administrative offices. The talent building, across the street, was where actors and movie directors were represented. If you wanted to break into the movie business, a role in the mailroom in the talent building was a prime job. Both buildings had dark windows—you could see out, but you couldn't see in. This made for great viewing, and I liked to observe the movie stars going in and out of that building.

At this point in my career, I didn't have a seat at the proverbial table. I was around executives and power brokers all the time, but they had no interest in talking to me unless they needed to use me as a conduit to my boss. I was invited into the C-suite for short bursts of time to either (a) drop off cups of coffee, (b) take meeting notes, or (c) refill the cups of coffee.

Still, I loved being in this Hollywood setting. Even though I was a rookie agent assistant, I was "in the building," which felt like a victory. Given my age and minimal corporate experience, I didn't mind being part of the background. Trying to fit into the corporate culture, I wore a nice black blazer. I wonder if anybody noticed that I wore the same blazer at least three days a week, every week. I didn't have the budget to buy business clothes at that time, let alone dry-clean them.

At work, nobody asked for my opinion, nor did I provide it to anybody. The exclusion felt normal in this environment where legendary agents were negotiating multimillion dollar deals. My boss was nice, though.

It was at the agency that I learned that everybody from the top to the bottom of the ladder used profanity easily and frequently. Dropping f-bombs was normal in this culture. I did so as well, and it helped me feel as if I fit in. I also felt that it helped punctuate the drama of a situation being discussed. For many years, I spoke with an abundance of profanity. It became natural.

At this early stage of my career, it appeared to me that men were in charge and had the leadership roles. Unfortunately, I wasn't exposed to many female role models or leaders during this time. The two women who held powerful positions at the agency had reputations for being tough bitches. I bought into that stereotype, believing that women could be in powerful roles but bitch status was required. This was naive of me.

I observed office arguments and a shocking altercation from the sidelines and tried to play it cool. I assumed that these behaviors were standard in the music industry—just regular drama. Now, I know better. Workplace violence of any kind is never okay. Report it immediately.

While I don't know what's happening in the music and talent agency industry these days, my journey has taken me to companies where I've seen more women in leadership roles. I've also taken it upon myself to pursue education and training on stereotypes, biases, and other important topics related to inclusion and opportunity.

***

While I was still working at the agency and living paycheck to paycheck, I became friends with an attorney who reviewed music contracts. He sat in an office next to my desk, and we'd occasionally chat about our hobbies. We came to learn that we both liked Rollerblading. He was older than I was by about ten years but still young enough to seem like a relatable friend. We agreed to meet up one weekend on the Santa Monica boardwalk, where we both liked to Rollerblade along the same path.

We had a fun time, and when our workout was over, we found a café and ordered lemonades at the counter. After ordering, he stepped back and walked away a little. I froze for a moment before pulling out my wallet. I had about ten dollars with me. Surely he'd treat me, the entry-level agent assistant, to the lemonade?

It turned out that he expected me to pay. At least that's how I read the situation. Not having the courage or know-how to say something, I bought the lemonades for both of us, just trying to play it cool, as if it were no sweat to hand over ten dollars. There went next week's spending money. I drove away thinking, *What a cheap fucker! He's an attorney for God's sake!* I was just trying to be cool, fit in, and have fun with a friend, not make a big deal. Even when my pocketbook was limited.

I shared this story with my younger son when we visited Santa Monica recently and gave him some advice: one should advocate for themselves and summon *self-worth* if they're not in a place to generously give. It's okay to ask someone to pay their share of the bill.

After a couple of years at the talent agency, I realized that I didn't want to be a music agent—or any other kind of agent. The whole Los Angeles scene seemed to be meant for rich and successful people. It was about status and who you knew. Certainly, having a job at this agency was a plus in my "LA standing," but my Mitsubishi Precis didn't quite hold a candle to the Mercedes, Bentleys, and Porsches in the agency parking garage. I couldn't exactly finance a luxury car while earning $8.65 per hour, and I was growing weary of Top Ramen dinners.

Eventually, a prospective boyfriend and ideas about a new career path took me north, to San Francisco.

REFLECTIONS ON LIFE

Below are journal-writing prompts that refer to themes I've shared in Part 1. There's no need to reflect on all of them. Choose one or a few. If you find the prompts helpful, come back and answer more. Sometimes focusing on one or two ideas at a time can help build momentum. Get curious about any insights that come up, and seek professional counseling or find a coach if you need deeper support.

Suggested journal-writing prompts:

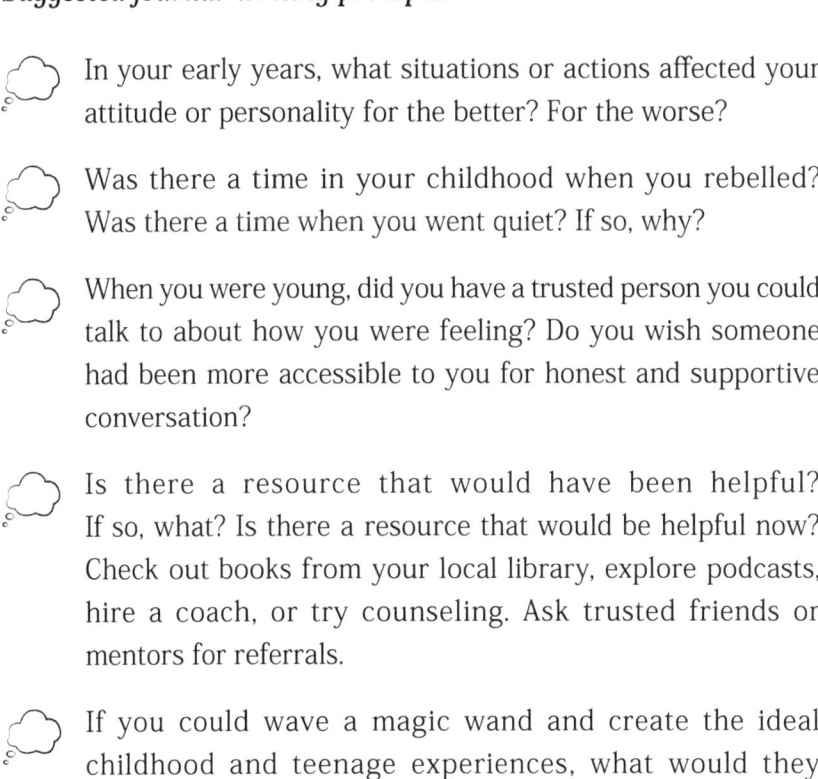

In your early years, what situations or actions affected your attitude or personality for the better? For the worse?

Was there a time in your childhood when you rebelled? Was there a time when you went quiet? If so, why?

When you were young, did you have a trusted person you could talk to about how you were feeling? Do you wish someone had been more accessible to you for honest and supportive conversation?

Is there a resource that would have been helpful? If so, what? Is there a resource that would be helpful now? Check out books from your local library, explore podcasts, hire a coach, or try counseling. Ask trusted friends or mentors for referrals.

If you could wave a magic wand and create the ideal childhood and teenage experiences, what would they have looked like?

What behaviors, actions, or attitudes, do you *not* want to carry with you into your future?

When you think about your future, what excites you? What makes you nervous or trepidatious?

What are you most grateful for in your life, and why?

What are the ways in which you take care of yourself now?

Where are you still looking to grow or evolve in terms of your behaviors, traits, or actions?

As I reflect on "Life," here are some of my key takeaways. I encourage you to contemplate these statements or consider making your own list.

Statements to empower you to make change:

- You can reinvent your life at any age, if you choose.
- You can make big, sweeping life changes and live through them.
- Dreams don't materialize overnight, but they do materialize if you stay the course and believe.
- Managing your mind is critical if you wish to both find peace and meet your goals.
- An abundance mindset is within your reach.

**Statements to remember
when you need a self-esteem boost:**

- You are worthy of having people in your life who treat you with kindness and authenticity.
- You don't have to live in chaos. You don't have to indulge in drama.
- You can keep your head high—always. Don't take anything personally. Keep moving forward and know that you are a worthy human being on this planet, regardless of others' actions toward you. Carry on.

*Anything can be changed,
fixed, or improved. At any age.*

PART 2: LOVE

Everyone you meet is a part of your journey,
but not all of them are meant to stay in your life.
Some people are just passing through to bring you
gifts; either they're blessings or lessons.

— Roy T. Bennett[5]

Relationships change. It's inevitable. Certain relationships in your life might no longer be supportive. You might be greatly disappointed by some. Perhaps surprised and delighted by others. And then there might be some that have evolved or expired.

I have a friend who is the dearest, most giving person I've ever known. A few years ago, this friend offered to help me pack up my house and move. I declined her offer, but she came anyway. She got on a plane to fly to my city and help me. Her gesture moved me to tears. Moving is no easy feat physically or mentally, and her loving action transcended friendship.

We've been friends since college, and I believe I've offered my friendship to her in the same way I've offered it to others. Why has she chosen to treat me well and stay consistent when certain others haven't?

Part 2 of this book is about love. Much of my focus in this part of the book is on relationships. What I've realized on my journey, though, is that self-love, my relationship with myself, is more important than I ever could have imagined. Self-love sounds quite corny. But there's something to it.

The fact that there are many layers to love and relationships has become clearer over the years as I become a more self-aware student of life.

I've had tremendous relationships for only a season of time. People have come and gone from my life either because I outgrew them or we outgrew each other. I've felt sad to see some friendships naturally dissolve over time due to distance or other factors, such as busy lives with demanding jobs and growing families, but life moves on.

At the end of the day, it's my choice to show up and accept or decline people's behaviors and treatment in relationships. I know this now.

Asking deeper questions of yourself is the first step to becoming aware of the dynamics in your relationships. You may one day come to realize that you no longer want to be available for people who disrespect you, flake on you, or are simply disengaged. Is there continued mutual interest in maintaining the relationship?

I've taken time to reflect on the behaviors that I chose to endure in relationships. In the past, accepting poor behavior in my marriage and long-term friendships made me feel supportive and loyal. I was being a "team player." But this was a learned behavior from my childhood. I'm wired to be loyal and show up, at times to my detriment. As I learned life skills and gained a stronger sense of my worth, though, I realized I no longer wanted to be on the receiving end of careless behaviors.

I held on to my failing marriage as an act of family survival, on behalf of my kids. Ultimately, it was an act of personal survival to leave.

In terms of my friendships, why was I putting up with friends who were constantly late and friends who flaked or canceled? *Did I set the expectations in these interactions?* I've wondered. Did I have to? Aren't we all adults? Can't we all show up with integrity and care and honor our commitments? We teach people how to treat us. As a friend, I don't want to coach anybody. I don't want to be someone's parent and tell them how they might want to treat people.

There comes a point when it's my decision to stay or go.

Why do we endure workplace relationships with people who (even with a smile on their face) oppress, micro-bully, snark, snicker, dismiss, or try to keep us in a container? I have a lot of "go along to get along" wired in me. I wasn't always good at articulating my confusion or discomfort in certain workplace interactions.

Here's the opportunity: we can make a different choice.

It was all a choice. The relationships I discuss in this book are relationships that I freely walked into and endured. I was willing to bend, twist, and disregard myself to keep relationships and dynamics going—out of love.

Then, it was my choice to turn the page and move on. What did this decision involve? Maturity. Greater self-awareness. Evolution. Growth. Courage.

Love.

11: THE JOURNAL

In my later years of college, I met someone who went to a school about an hour from mine, and we dated long-distance. He was a cute surfer-type with smarts. And his own car. He served a purpose for my ego, but as my needs and values began evolving in my early twenties, I could see that he didn't meet my longer-term dating standards. Eventually, the dynamic was no longer easy and fun. We started bickering. I'd complain about his lack of ambition. He'd complain about my complaining.

You can't change someone. I know that now.

My loyalty runs deep, and it can be difficult for me to let go and comprehend that I'll be okay. At that time of my life, it was impossible for me to understand that I could move through the upset of a loss. How do you walk away from love, even when a relationship has expired? It seemed as if the pain would be insurmountable. Hanging on felt logical and safe. The possibility of a bright rainbow on the other side of loss wasn't a concept I'd been made aware of.

After I graduated from college we broke up, and months afterward, I had an early morning dream. I was in bed with a man who had a very nice physique. I was sleeping behind him and had my arm wrapped over his shoulder. It felt like someone new. Someone who was coming to me. I remember so clearly waking up and feeling an energy shift. My college ex seemed distant. I had a huge smile on my face and a refreshed attitude. I could energetically feel a new man headed my way.

***

Fast-forward to June 2020. I was cleaning my garage and came across old boxes of personal belongings. One of these items was a journal from when I was twenty-five years old. Most of the entries were about a guy I'd recently met—the guy who would, years later, become my husband and the father of my two kids: Tom.

The journal entries described the early days of our knowing each other. I detailed just how cute I thought this guy was. Physical attractiveness was still very important to me in a relationship, based on the societal norms I'd internalized in my childhood.

The journal also revealed to me how I was getting played by him, although I couldn't see it then. He'd call me sometimes. He'd occasionally tell me how great I was and then ghost me. I saw long-term potential. He was cute and seemed successful, so I hung on. No, I *clawed* on.

As I skimmed through the journal, I reflected. *Who was I at 25?* I was a girl smitten with an alluring boy. A girl feeling insecure about this new relationship because he'd go silent. A girl with solid intuition who felt that this boy was dating his ex-girlfriend again (or maybe they were never fully broken up) but who ignored that gut feeling. He'd bait me with kind, sweet words and then cast me off, only to try to reel me in again. I so wanted to be reeled in.

These were the days before social media, so there was no peeking in on someone through their online activity. I could only guess, stress, ponder, and despair over where he was and why he wasn't calling me.

After one particularly stressful and lonely weekend of not hearing from him, I decided to call his house on Sunday night. The answering machine picked up. I paused. *Should I just hang up? Or share a piece of my mind?* I decided on the latter.

After the beep I said, "Hi, it's Kate. I hope you had a great weekend. And by the way, if you're attempting to be an asshole, you've succeeded." Click.

Straightforward. Still, why had I allowed myself to get caught up in a quagmire of frustration and desperation? Why didn't I just move on if he *was* attempting to be an asshole? Riddle me that.

As I've said, people will show you who they are. Believe them. At this time in my life, I was too emotionally immature to accept that this guy was showing me who he was. I didn't get it.

Instead of being offended, he found my voice message funny, thrilling, and memorable—he remembered it for years. I truly captured his attention. He seemed to perk up after that and veer from whatever other lanes he'd been in into mine.

It felt like a victory. Really, it was a red flag. I liked to pursue the elusive guys, the guys whose interest I had to work a little harder to keep.

Sitting cross-legged on the ground of my garage, I felt sick to my stomach as I read the journal, revisiting my days as young Kate. I could vividly recall those feelings of hope and desperation, of hanging on, moment by moment, waiting for the phone to ring. Uncertainty would pulse through me as I tried to decipher each missing-in-action situation.

If only I were as wise then as I am now, I thought.

But wisdom is gained on the battle ground. I could see glimmers of my keen intuition pointing me in the right direction, but I chose to ignore them. Deep down, I knew things weren't quite right. But he was attractive and seemed more sophisticated than people I had dated before. I so badly wanted to be wanted by a cute guy who had that air of maturity and slight mystery.

I've felt compelled to write this romantic tale before, but the timing wasn't right until now. I first needed all the revelations I gained by way of exploring my inner-child wounds. At this stage of my life, I'm more aware of why I chose the person I chose, why I continued to stay despite red flags, and what I learned over many years of finally being honest with myself.

Without reading all the entries, I threw the journal into the outdoor trash can then paused. *Should I save this for my kids? Should I grab it out of there and hide it somewhere for a later date? Should I show them the raw story of the beginning of their parents' almost twenty-year relationship?*

The person who'd written in that journal was naive. Desperate. Standing by the trash can, I reflected on how I'd ignored the signs and become an unwitting victim of my own emotional immaturity. Decision made. I wouldn't retrieve the historical journal from the trash.

I had turned the page. In fact, the page had been turned for many years. The sadness of a lost relationship, of lost love, and then divorce might never fully go away, especially when children are involved. But it gets better. Way better.

I resolved instead to share my revelations by way of this book. This way, my kids would see the sad parts and also, more importantly, the diamond that keeps getting brighter and brighter.

12: THE GUY

Despite the free concert tickets available to me through my job in LA, my weekends had become somewhat lonely, and I often felt isolated. One long weekend holiday, I decided to fly up to my parents' house to spend some time with them.

A good friend from college had moved to my hometown, and she wanted to go out on Saturday night, so we ventured downtown. We were at a bar when one of our friends met a few guys who said they were moving on to a different bar. My friends wanted to go with them. I wasn't in the mood to caravan to a different bar but went ahead and followed them, annoyed. The new bar ended up being lively and full of people our age.

At one point, I noticed a guy standing behind the group of people I was talking to. *Who's THAT guy?* I thought. What I said out loud was "Who's your friend back there?" Soon, I was chatting with him.

I felt an inkling that I knew him from another time and place. He felt familiar, for sure. We chatted until the bar closed and then exchanged phone numbers.

He called my house phone that night. Well, my parents' house phone. My dad sleepily and angrily answered the call. I was tickled. A boy calling my house late at night felt so high school. So fun. I told him that I'd be back in Los Angeles on Sunday and that he was welcome to call me there. And he did, before I got home. He left a message with my roommate. More excitement.

After that, Tom and I began a long-distance conversation. Soon, our conversations involved the prospect of traveling to see one another. He tried to entice me to visit him first, in his town, telling me about the really fun weekend we'd have. He suggested that I fly up, but funds in my bank account were extremely low. I did have a credit card . . .

My hesitancy prompted him to offer to pay for my flight. *Wow!* I felt special. He wanted to plan a special weekend for me *and* pay for my flight. He seemed as if he had it together, and that was appealing to me. At the ripe age of twenty-four, I was looking for potential-husband material, and he appeared to be checking important boxes. We did have a wonderful and fun weekend, but he never paid me for the flight I booked on my credit card. I never said anything. It seemed too awkward to ask. Maybe he'd just forgotten? I shoved down my disappointment (and credit card bill) and instead, gushed to myself about what a great prospect he was.

After a year of dating him long-distance, I decided to quit my job in Los Angeles and move to the Bay Area. I reasoned that my long-term career prospects didn't lie in the music industry. It seemed to me that it was older men who succeeded in this industry. Although the music world was fun, it was also extremely competitive, and that didn't speak to me. The LA vibe was all about status—where you worked, who you knew, where you lived, what kind of car you drove. My trusty stick-shift Mitsubishi Precis and I weren't entirely rocking the scene.

I couldn't see the career path in music. I couldn't see the endgame. I couldn't see my new boyfriend!

I had already put in my notice at the agency when the manager of a famous comedian visited my boss. We'd become friendly, so I told her I'd resigned and would be pursuing a career in network television in the Bay Area. She paused, looked at me quizzically, and said, "Honey, the television jobs are in LA. But good luck."

Bay Area here I come!

Tom and I decided to move in together after one year of dating. I found us an impressive two-bedroom flat in an incredible neighborhood in San Francisco, and we began living together with no commitments or promises. I didn't even think about discussing shared understandings or goals. I figured that our living together sealed some kind of deal and the relationship would progress toward marriage in due time.

Dr. Laura Schlessinger hosts a daily radio show, and one important topic she speaks about is relationships.[6] I found her radio show after I had kids. When I started tuning in, I learned that she often shares a particular point of view about unmarried couples living together. Had I called in during my dating and living-together days, she likely would have told me that we were not, in fact, blissfully living together—we were "shacking up" and that I was "a woman being used." I'd never considered this perspective before. Nobody had shared it with me.

Her stark declaration came too late for me to consider. And if I'd heard her say this when I was in my midtwenties, I probably would have been offended and brushed off the criticism.

I'm older and wiser now and can now understand the point she was making: marital commitment is the conduit to bringing two lives together under one roof. At the time, I was making decisions that I believed an independent and empowered woman would make.

I'd gotten myself into a situation where there were no rules, no boundaries, no promises between us. I was naive and thrilled to be adulting so awesomely. I'd made it. Living with an attractive boyfriend: check. Playing the role of adult: check.

Living in that moment, I felt as if I'd leveled up in my dating capability. My new boyfriend made me feel as though I were dating a mature adult. He was two and a half years older than I was. We spent our free time dining out at local hot spots and having drinks together, which felt very cultured to me. We had interests in common and enjoyed each other's company. He became a best friend.

I was living my dream.

***

Have you considered your deepest values and how you honor yourself when making big life decisions?

I can see now that my decision to move in with someone (regardless of whether we were married or not) needed to involve expectations, agreements, and timelines that were clear to both people. The decision to cohabitate shouldn't be made based on the assumption that someone will propose, someday.

I encourage you not to just show up and play house without mutual agreements. If you are coming together under one roof, there are elementary yet mature conversations that need to be had. Who's paying the bills? Is the higher income earner paying more? Who's responsible for what household duties? There are so many disasters waiting to happen when you try to take a romantic, time-will-tell approach to a very adult situation. Today, I'd tell myself not to simply wing it with my future and hope for the best.

Having limited maturity about adult agreements, Tom and I ended up with an unwritten, haphazard way of paying our shared bills. We each wrote checks for precisely 50 percent of our rent. For ten years, we turned in two checks to our landlord. I'd assumed that he'd want to take care of the utilities and other bills—after all, wasn't I dating a successful man? Then again, I was an independent woman. Hear me roar and watch me take out my checkbook.

When he forgot to pay bills and the late-payment notices came, I went ahead and took charge. Overdue notices made me anxious. Responsible, do-gooder Kate wanted to step up and take care of business. I'd then tell him how much he owed me for his half of the bills. He either wouldn't believe me or would argue that he'd already paid me back for that bill. Arguments about money ensued. Monthly. So, I began keeping a bills log. It lived in a drawer by our house phone. I had to start micromanaging his paying me back. Over the years (and I can only see this in hindsight), I was unknowingly behaving like a parent figure. Taking care of business.

It was frustrating trying to change his approach. My path of least resistance was to step in and fix. I shouldn't have done that. When someone shows you who they are, believe them.

Not long after we moved in together, Tom encountered a financial challenge and needed my help. He asked for my credit card, saying he needed to borrow six hundred dollars. In my midtwenties, I was just getting my career started and was working good jobs, but my earnings were modest. I was living paycheck to paycheck and my credit card was for emergencies. It had a credit limit of no more than a few thousand dollars. Nonetheless, I didn't think twice about letting him use it. I didn't ask what his issue or challenge was. I just wanted to be sweet, helpful, and loving. He told me that he'd pay off the credit card. I believed him. I never checked the bill when it came in. He never paid it. The letters and phone calls from bill collectors seeking their six hundred dollars plus interest finally caught my attention, and I realized what was happening. There were excuses and explanations on his end: "There must have been a misunderstanding."

In the end, I went ahead and paid off the entire debt. I was upset, and he knew it. I felt that it was important to keep my credit rating in good standing. At least I was a team player and a supportive girlfriend. That was my mission. People-pleasing. Codependency. Just sweep it under the carpet, Kate.

The relationship was fun and games. We took trips to Napa for wine tastings. We'd go to Carmel. Spend a weekend in Tahoe. When we were at home, we'd go out drinking at bars in San Francisco. We'd cook dinner together and watch TV shows.

Many months after settling into our San Francisco apartment, we went out for dinner and drinks with a few other couples. We were seated at a large round table. Conversation was flowing, and I made a comment I thought was innocent. Tom, apparently, thought differently. He snapped at me and made me feel like a child. Silence descended. People glanced at each other and at me with expressions of surprise and pity. I didn't know what to do, what to say, so I shrank in my chair, blushing. After dinner, the party moved on but I decided to go home. Riding in the cab, I felt alone and ashamed. I should have broken up with him right then. Nobody with healthy self-worth, self-love, or self-esteem would have allowed themselves to be treated that way. Candidly, a red flag was ignored.

I started normalizing feeling as if I was being spoken to condescendingly. Telling myself that these interactions were simply misunderstandings or small arguments, I'd go quiet and just move on. External observers saw something different. This wasn't respectful, loving behavior in a relationship.

As we evolve, we must audit and reaudit our needs. During my childhood, I felt as if I couldn't advocate for myself, and this was normalized. As I entered adulthood, I didn't have the awareness to determine what respectful, mature conversation in a relationship looked like. I wondered why conversations often led to conflict. With my parents as my biggest relationship models, I hadn't observed how to calmly resolve conflict. I didn't know how to ensure that my needs were being heard and met.

I now know that enduring disrespect isn't normal. It's not team-player behavior. Figure out how you want to be treated—and find people who treat you that way.

13: CAREER LIFE

When I moved to the Bay Area, a friend who worked at a temp agency asked if I'd be willing to work a few temp jobs while looking for an ideal job. I agreed, needing to earn money.

One such job changed my career trajectory. It was at a Silicon Valley biotech firm, and I was a fish out of water, having just come out of the flashy LA music scene. I was placed in the human resources department. My boss was a cool young woman who was interested in all things Ireland. She decided to start calling me Katie—because it felt more Irish to her. I went with it. My work involved doing a lot of filing and working with personnel files, which I found fascinating. It was the first time I got a glimpse of what moving up the career ladder could look like financially because I was viewing salaries in the files. I could see what was possible. I was shocked to see what the chief HR officer was earning in base salary—in the 200K range.

Early in my career, I'd heard that for every one year of experience, you earn ten thousand dollars in salary. I figured that twenty years of labor would get me to a jackpot of two hundred thousand a year. *The chief HR officer seems about fifty years old,* I thought. *Only twenty-five more years of work and maybe I can get to her level of compensation.*

I became intrigued by the possibility of a career in HR, finding the various aspects of the work and the interactions with people quite interesting. I didn't stay at the biotech firm, though. It wasn't the right cultural fit for me. In the music-industry job, I'd identified that working in a creative industry was rewarding to me. I still feel the same way.

I ended up finding an incredible job as a human resources coordinator at a global advertising agency. When I went in for the interview, I was blown away. The place was swarming with young and vibrant people. And many of these people had window offices. *What?!*

In the music industry, older men had the window offices. I'd believed older workers were smarter because they'd paid their dues. That was my paradigm. The ad agency turned that on its side (not quite upside down). I felt as if I'd entered a candy store with its bright colors and yumminess. The views from the office building were incredible. The agency took up three floors of the high-rise and you could see for miles in all directions. I was awed by the views of the Bay Bridge, Golden Gate Bridge, Alcatraz, the Berkeley Hills, and so much more. My gut told me that I'd found a home where I'd love to stay for a long while.

I grew to learn that big career opportunities *were* available to younger people—you just had to find the right door to go through. At the ad agency, younger people had big job titles and big responsibilities. It was eye-opening to see the younger demographic lead teams, run meetings, and act as key decision-makers. Maybe I was eligible for this too. I wasn't sure how, but I seemed to be in the right place to learn.

My boss is still a friend to this day. I applied my thoughts and ideas to the work, and she taught me to believe that they were good. She praised me for taking a project and making it even better. She trusted me fully with the company internship program, which I designed and ran. Her support and trust were a confidence booster at this point in my career.

When you land a good boss, be thankful. Nurture that relationship. Ask questions and listen closely. Get feedback—more on this later.

My boss also taught me that it was okay to use my voice. In fact, it was encouraged. She invited me to meetings and expected me to speak. This was new and uncomfortable, and it took practice after working in a "be seen but not heard" role in LA.

In my early days in this job, my boss invited me to an HR team off-site conference in Chicago. It was fun to see colleagues from our other offices. Sitting around the conference room table with everyone was informative—as well as intimidating. I didn't feel qualified to contribute to the conversation. A limiting belief crept in: *I haven't paid my dues.* My boss kindly called my quiet demeanor to my attention after the first day of the conference. This was one of the earliest pieces of performance feedback I'd ever received. Learning to feel worthy and knowledgeable enough to speak up and share was a years-long process.

Through reflection, I've realized that I received most of my primary education in a lecture style. I was talked to and expected to sit quietly and listen. Rarely were students engaged in dialogue and critical-thinking exercises. Thus, speaking up didn't feel natural. I hadn't been trained for that.

In addition to the feedback from my boss to *use* my voice, I still hold on to a piece of advice I received from a music-industry boss and informal mentor. He had a wise, calm demeanor and was pleasant to work with. "Kate," he said one day, "let me teach you something." After a long pause, he said, "Keep your eyes open, keep your ears open, and keep your mouth shut." The importance of *listening* stuck with me, and I took his advice seriously. It has turned out to be sage wisdom not just in my career but in my life in general. I've made it a point to become better and better at listening. Actively listening. Seeking to understand people. Listening is a skill that managers and employees alike can benefit from growing and nurturing.

***

At the ad agency, my cubicle was built like a large phone booth, with windows on three sides of me. To my right and behind me, I could see downtown San Francisco. To my left, I could see Coit Tower and the Bay. Sitting in this cube in this high-rise building made me feel as if I'd "made it" in my career.

I was doing fun work, with a fun boss and team. I was learning a lot and enjoying being in a corporate ecosystem. Working in the HR department, I also helped people who had resigned transition out of the company. Each resignation from this fabulous place shook me. Where was their loyalty? Didn't they care about the company as much as I did? I mean, this was an incredible place to work!

These individuals typically moved on to other ad-agency jobs for better titles and higher pay. Eventually, the resignations stopped fazing me. I was learning about the cycle of employment: build your résumé and gain experience while waiting for the next career-advancing opportunity that pays more money, then leave. I understood this to be a ladder-climbing game, and it made sense.

Then one day, my boss resigned. Same story. She was moving on to a new, bigger job that paid more. Her resignation made me sad. I also wondered who would guide me now.

By way of HR department attrition, I found myself alone in the department and being called up to the C-suite to interact and work with executives. This felt exciting and right. I knew with every fiber of my being that I was in my zone. I was where I needed to be based on my overall aspirations. I was ready for a ladder-climbing adventure. However, I was insecure about my lack of corporate experience.

The executives wanted my expertise and my opinions, and I just didn't have the training or years of experience to be informative or influential yet. What I learned in this early stage of my career, though, was that I could exude an air of confidence and be a great listener. I could emulate gravitas. My advice to myself, as I sat in these rooms, was to act as if I belonged there. I could also be honest and let them know when I needed to research and investigate matters that I was unsure of. I believed this to be a reasonable response.

During my younger years of interacting with senior leaders and establishing my presence, I developed my professionalism. I was always dependable when it came to my deliverables, and I built trust when interacting with others.

Gaining experience and know-how takes time. Similar to working out at the gym, you have to get in the "reps" to get better and stronger. As I look back on my career, I recall that I've held thousands of 1:1 meetings and attended thousands of meetings—all these interactions build skills and expertise. Over time you start to realize that you are, in fact, the subject matter on any number of topics. For me, I can't walk out of a complex training and wield those skills immediately. It takes time to assess the new skills, integrate, and practice.

Sometimes you need to get thrown in the deep end to accelerate personal progress. I didn't naturally steer myself toward public speaking opportunities. When speaking called, I was forced to plan, prepare. and then just do it. As my career progressed, I knew I needed to voluntarily do more public speaking, and it finally became easier. Hearty pep talks are definitely part of the success formula.

14: RED FLAGS

My maternal grandmother died in her eighties after enduring various illnesses for decades. She lived a modest, if not impoverished, life in Scotland. We exchanged letters when I was growing up. A few months after my granny passed away, my mom told me that she'd left me a small monetary gift: $1,500. I was shocked that she'd died with anything to her name and received the gift with great gratitude, understanding its significance both to her and to me. At the time, $1,500 was a large amount of money for me.

I shared this news with Tom, who suggested that I invest the money. In fact, he said he could help me open an investment fund at the small brokerage firm he worked at (not as a licensed broker). He talked a lot about the stock market and the upside to investing. I went ahead and opened an account with his firm and deposited my money, and allowed him to allocate it to different stocks. The market was hot at the time. Tech stocks were on the move. I didn't discuss my investment goals with him. I just assumed the money would sit there and go up in value over time.

Having online access to the account, I'd occasionally check the status of my money and noticed that he was frequently buying and selling different stocks on my behalf. *He's smart and experienced in the stock market*, I told myself. I trusted his decisions with my money and didn't question his investing tactics. I believed that he'd protect my precious gift.

About eighteen months later, the account had bottomed out and was worth zero. I was angry and ashamed, and I berated myself for my lack of knowledge and lack of desire to understand the stock market so that I could take over the investment. My granny's money was gone, and it felt like a gut punch. That experience was eye-opening. I couldn't trust others with my money. Period. I had to hold myself accountable.

"I'm not good with money" or "I don't like dealing with money" aren't valid excuses. Your money is your responsibility. Get educated about how to manage it, even if this simply means mastering the basics (saving, interest rates, etc.). Money management will never be an advanced or favorite activity for me, but if I'm not going to manage my money carefully and smartly, how can I expect more money to flow to me?

I've done a great deal of money-mindset work over the last few years. Doing so is important if you want to open up to the possibilities of having more money flow in your direction. I'll elaborate on this later.

***

Tom and I dated for eight years before getting married. During those eight years of dating, I was wishing and praying that we could just get married and begin a fantasy life. So many of our friends were getting married and starting families. We attended the weddings of most of the people in our different friend circles, and I felt like the last one in line. I was hanging on. Waiting. Wondering. Stressing. Dreaming. Analyzing. Sad. Hopeful. Embarrassed.

I hadn't yet heard of Dr. Laura and her pointed relationship advice. However, I'd heard the joke about "not buying the milk when you can have the cow for free." It made me feel a little defensive, but I didn't think it applied to me.

During the later years of our dating, I sought counseling from a couple of different therapists when I needed clarity about the relationship and was pondering the roadblocks. In hindsight, I wonder why one of these therapists didn't alert me more emphatically to the signs of dysfunction, and why no one spoke candidly to me about potential options and the pros and cons of each option. My therapists were nice, and it was lovely that they gave me books to read about alcoholism and codependency, but I felt that these books simply didn't apply to me. I didn't need to learn about alcoholism or things of that nature. I had marriage goals. Period.

I didn't have the self-awareness and courage to be truthful with myself about the long-term implications of continuing in this relationship. I was laser focused on my short-term wants—I wanted a road map to the ring.

My therapists usually put conversations about alcoholism on our agenda, but my mind always went back to the same conclusion—these were other people's problems, not mine. I don't think anybody talked to me about the potential outcomes of being in a relationship where both addiction and antagonism were present. If they did, the message didn't get through to me. Nobody asked me if I observed patterns in my own relationship that were similar to those in my parents' marriage.

To me, it seemed as if Tom and I just needed to stop continually arguing and to get engaged. It was hard to see beyond that.

I wanted this relationship so much. I was immersed in our friendship, our love, and my attraction to him. I wanted a diamond ring and a storybook wedding. I wanted the dream. Reality was showing me red flags, and I couldn't grasp it. I was a hang-in-there kind of girl and believed that any outcome other than a proposal would mean I'd failed.

My counseling didn't click on the lightbulb. I didn't have a mentor or guidebook, though I could have used one. I didn't know the terminology for what our relationship consisted of. I didn't know the words. I didn't know the dynamics. Nobody taught me or revealed textbook definitions of toxic behaviors in a relationship, and what that might look or feel like. I was self-righteous, indignant, and independent. At that time—and for most of my life—I felt I had plenty of self-love, self-respect, and self-worth. If only I'd had the necessary information to empower myself and comprehend the reality of being in a relationship that wasn't peaceful or respectful.

I finally sounded my own alarm bells in the summer of 2001. The relationship just wasn't working. There were too many tearful nights, too many fights that were getting more difficult to work through. At this point, Tom would leave the house for hours or days at a time, to escape from our issues.

What are we doing? I'd wonder. *Where is this going? Why can't lifestyle decisions change? Greater happiness and ease could be ours, if each of us were free and clear in our mind and body.* These questions and musings made me "difficult" and "overbearing" and "needy."

Conversations about the future weren't fruitful. Yes, we talked about marriage, but he would allude to not being ready. The relationship had no defined goals or vision. His thoughts were shorter term, mostly looking to the weekend ahead. The reality of the relationship was front and center. I wasn't emotionally mature enough to accept it. I wasn't mature enough to understand that to envision the path ahead, I only had to look at past behaviors.

I thought about breaking up all the time. A state of angst and despair is not a healthy place to be. I vented and sought solace with friends, who encouraged me to hang in there. Nobody raised concerns or doubts—except for my parents, who grew to become upset about how I was feeling. Despite my hurt, I always defended him.

My concerns about breaking up were shortsighted. I didn't contemplate a future bursting with opportunities and possibilities. Instead, I wondered how I'd cover the rent by myself if we broke up. My narrow mind couldn't comprehend how I'd be able to pay an extra six hundred dollars every month.

At this point, I'd never considered my money mindset. I didn't realize it was a thing. I just accepted my bimonthly paycheck and called it a day. As mentioned earlier, I felt more money would come in future decades. These days, there are many books and podcasts that provide excellent information about money mindset. No matter your age, if you don't believe that you can change your financial trajectory, I urge you to investigate your money mindset.[7]

After almost eight years of dating, Tom and I made the big decision to break up. He went to go live with a friend. This time, we wouldn't ignore each other for a week and then make up. We'd had numerous stops and starts in communication while living together, but this time, we truly intended to end it. In my mind, it was over once and for all. We didn't have contact for a few weeks. It felt lonely and I was in the depths of pain, but I was taking it day by day. Doing better incrementally.

Then the national crisis of 9/11 happened, and our mutual fear led us back to each other. We talked on the phone that morning, both worried about the state of the world. We rushed to be together and console each other as the nation seemed to be falling apart. Life felt so fragile at that time. Would life, the country, ever be the same again?

A month after 9/11, we met for lunch and had a deep conversation on a park bench. We were kind of back together but hadn't discussed the status of the relationship. He was reflective about life and pledged to make behavioral adjustments in some areas. We wanted to find a way to make this relationship work. Our history and love were a gravitational pull.

In that park, we decided that marriage was the next step. I mean, when the world is falling apart, why not make a major life decision?

Obviously, I'm being sarcastic. Fear is a poor place from which to make decisions. Today, I would tell my younger self to go to couples counseling with him. After all, we'd broken up for good reasons. Yes, there was history and love there, but were we really a match? It needed deeper exploration.

At this point, though, I wanted to have the kind of wedding that every bride dreams of. After eight years of dating, I felt that I deserved it. I read tons of bridal magazines and ripped out pages to help storyboard the vision of my wedding. I crafted a beautiful wedding canvas. Nine months after our conversation in the park, we exchanged vows in front of seventy-five people in beautiful Santa Barbara—a destination wedding. And I paid for it. Well, my parents generously contributed too. Neither of his (divorced) parents attended the wedding. The state of his (and my) relationship with his parents didn't bother me at the time.

Family dynamics are important components of a relationship. Extended family is a reality, and it's important to be honest with yourself about the state of those relationships (or lack thereof). How will you navigate them and support your partner? Will your partner have your back during family encounters? Premarital counseling might be advisable to explore this. I encourage you to reflect on family realities and expectations.

Truth and transparency are needed—and not just when it comes to extended family.

15: UNRAVELING

Tom and I discussed having kids during our dating years and while engaged. We knew that we wanted them. There was even a boy's name that we'd been discussing for years, and it was a fun topic of conversation.

What we didn't discuss were the ultra-important topics, such as who would stay home and raise the children, who would provide the health-care benefits, and whether we should create a joint financial fund for baby expenses. We just knew we wanted kids. Once again, I felt as if things would just work themselves out—for the best.

We had our first child in April 2003, and our baby was just magical. Such a blessing.

Looking after a new baby was an out-of-body experience. A newborn takes over every moment of your day. Life as I knew it was over. My attention was on this perfect little creature. Being a new mom was joyful but also isolating, especially in our neighborhood in San Francisco, where there weren't other families and kids.

I always knew that I wanted two children. I enjoyed the friendship and companionship I had with my brother and believed that a two-kid family would be perfect for me. And so, one and a half years after having our first son, I got pregnant with our second child.

In February 2006, we decided that living in San Francisco no longer suited our family. City living just couldn't accommodate this party of four. With two very young kids in tow, we moved out of our 1100-square-foot flat in San Francisco and into a fixer-upper in the East Bay suburbs.

Our fixer house underwent months of massive construction and design work. The time, money, and patience that the ongoing work required put tremendous strain on our relationship. The project was huge and never seemed to be done. With two children needing most of my attention, I deferred most decisions about the house to Tom. I appreciated his intent to make the place more livable and comfortable, but there was never a substantive conversation, let alone a mutual agreement, about project scope or budget.

I'll share it again: transparent conversations and agreements are a necessary part of being a couple, a family. Alignment is important too. Even though I was distracted by the children, I was interested in the other important things going on. Still, I felt that the path of least resistance was not asking too many questions. This helped keep the peace.

If you think having clarifying or alignment conversations will lead to arguments, get into individual or couples counseling and have someone help you. Operating within mutual agreements is so important.

***

When I was pregnant with our first son, I accepted a one-off job working for the wife of the CEO of a large consumer retailer company. The job was a means to an end while I was pregnant and between HR jobs. By way of that job, I got a glimpse of massive wealth: their mansion in Pacific Heights, hired help, invitations from celebrities and socialites, travels by private jet. My job was to help with the administrative details of an important cancer-awareness gala that she was hosting. She received permission to host the gala inside the San Francisco Ferry Building. Shortly after the gala, I had my baby and didn't return to this job.

About one year later, I took another HR job in an advertising agency. During my interview with this agency, the HR leader asked me, "So, what do you like to do for fun?" I didn't have an answer to that question—I was completely caught off guard. With a young baby at home, I was operating in mom-mode and didn't have time to have fun. I took a few beats before giving her a song-and-dance answer that I might have given years prior.

Despite feeling off my interview game, I was offered the job. It felt great to be back in the advertising world, in the HR seat. The job was within walking distance of my house, which felt reassuring for me with the baby at home. Tom was out of a job at that time, so he became the baby's caretaker during my workday.

When I was preparing to go on maternity leave with my second son, I knew I needed to train my team—my HR manager in particular. I wanted her to establish herself as the HR authority in my absence. I thought back to my early days in HR, when I was the most senior HR team member at the company and designing my own ways to establish authority.

I coached her on acting as if she belonged in every room, and on how to establish her executive presence. We talked about how to reply to questions when you don't know the answer. I felt confident that she was up to the task of covering for me, and sure enough, when I returned from my leave, I could see that her confidence had elevated to an exciting level. She'd established her presence and made a wonderful mark in my absence. In fact, she'd increased her experience to the extent that she got recruited away to another job. I was proud of her.

After having my second child, I knew that nine-to-five corporate life would be too challenging for me. I wanted more time with my kids. That was my priority. Yet, I was in a situation that required me to work and earn income for my family.

This was a pivotal point for me. I was enjoying career success. My husband, with his commissions-based job, was seemingly unable to be the primary breadwinner after we had our children. There were a lot of assumptions made by both of us at this time about the family operation. I loved my career and being able to provide my HR expertise in the workplace. I was highly employable. He wasn't in that space. Initially, I saw his lack of career stability as my opportunity to continue growing my career and bringing in the money. That path seemed prudent.

Still, I wanted something different. I had to audit my needs. Among my needs and values were time and freedom, and these were speaking loudly to me. I deeply desired to spend more time with my children, and to have the freedom to create my own schedule. My values guided me to walk away from full-time corporate employment after a few years at the ad agency. Time was going to be my most precious commodity. The money would have to find a way in.

With two kids needing our focus, Tom and I had canceled or delayed so many conversations and decisions about our finances and careers. There was no plan. What happened next is that life slowly became "every spouse for themselves" in terms of financial survival.

Here I go again! Family agreements are critical, and they should ideally be made *before* you begin building a family. I suggest designing a road map that creates clarity and understanding regarding how each adult in the family will own and deliver desired outcomes. Who works? Who stays home? Is there a hybrid? What happens if the primary income earner stops earning money? How much money is needed to support the family? What happens if a career takes a multiyear hiatus?

This might not seem romantic. It doesn't matter. Life responsibilities aren't romantic. They're tangible and real. Assumptions shouldn't be made. Have both eyes open. Lack of planning can easily end in a difficult or distressing situation.

I was fortunate to find an incredible job after leaving the "big corporate job." It required me to be at the office twenty hours per week, and the commute was reasonable. I stayed there for seven years. I was able to take on a rewarding body of work building out an entire HR infrastructure for a company that I admired—all while I was hands-on raising my children. I was paid well, but there came a point where it wasn't enough. I took on an entrepreneurial pursuit in addition to my part-time job.

As the months and years wore on, Tom and I lived in a loop of arguments and misunderstandings. Alignment on issues seemed impossible. Part of my growing coping strategy was to cut conversations short or avoid them altogether. When I disengaged from conversations, we seemed to recover from the drama more quickly. How could communication be so strenuous? I couldn't crack the code.

One evening, we got into yet another disagreement. It was bedtime for the kids, so I stepped away and began my peaceful nighttime routine of rocking my youngest son to sleep. About twenty minutes later, Tom flung open the door to our son's room and loudly said, "The police are at the front door looking for you!" Then he stormed out.

Not only did this sudden and aggressive declaration scare the hell out of me, it also frightened our son. I took a moment to assess the situation and determined that Tom was lying. I knew he was trying to push my buttons. However, I regularly felt gaslit at that point, so my mind rapidly searched for reasons why the police *could* be there. Of course, there weren't police at the door. I didn't even get up to look outside. It was another case of him antagonizing me. Really, it went beyond antagonizing.

This is the strongest story that I'll share about feeling like I was enduring toxic behavior.

There were more encounters. One story like this is too many. Still, it was difficult to think about ending a relationship when there were children involved. I was going to hang in there on behalf of my kids. I felt I had to.

I've heard it said that it takes more strength to know when to let go of something than to hang on to it. This was certainly true for me. Breaking up a family is a terrible thing to consider. But when you're on the receiving end of behaviors that are neither respectful nor safe, I urge you to seek professional help and explore your options for exiting the situation safely.

16: INNER GUIDANCE

Many of my mentors are TV hosts or authors. I once believed that "proper" mentors had to be people you knew personally. I want to bust that myth. Smart strangers can have a profound and positive impact on you. I've written Oprah three times to thank her. Her teachings have helped me. No, she hasn't written back.

If you're lucky enough to have in-person mentors, congratulations. If you don't, find an author or impactful podcast to follow. Seek information from any positive and helpful source.

I came to know one of my TV mentors during the later parts of my marriage. I experienced many dark nights in our bedroom by myself. On Saturday nights, I'd watch *The Suze Orman Show* on MSNBC, my favorite show at the time. I'd listen intently as Suze provided no-nonsense financial advice, which was crucial for me at the time. The show taught me to get smarter about my finances and financial planning.

The other show I found invaluable at the time was *Til Debt Do Us Part*, hosted by Gail Vaz-Oxlade. She'd analyze people's bank accounts and expenditures and would often recommend that they get a second or supplementary job to create more income. This concept was eye-opening. It dawned on me that I didn't have to be held captive by what *one* employer paid me.

I started to contemplate my limiting beliefs. I was choosing to be fully dependent on one income source with one employer. Why couldn't I increase my overall earnings by way of multiple income streams?

I'd also never really analyzed how many times I swiped my debit cards in one day, which the show made clear to me. Why hadn't I thought about my spending in this way before? These shows helped me become more financially savvy as I planned my next chapters.

I recorded the final episode of Oprah's TV show and watched it one night in my dark cave of a bedroom. During one of the segments, Oprah talked about life speaking to you in whispers. The whispers might get louder, and then life might begin to yell at you. If you still don't pay attention, then a brick wall will fall on you, trying desperately to get you to listen to the message.[8]

I had a massive aha moment watching this episode. The whispers had come and gone. The bricks had landed. Though I'd tried to push it down and manage it, the stress in my marriage had impacted me. The metaphorical bricks were all over me—mentally, physically, spiritually.

In the final years of my marriage, I was diagnosed with a variety of medical issues. I was hanging tough, but my body was stressed out and trying to tell me. In the decade that's passed since my divorce, I haven't had any health conditions on that level.

If you're experiencing both relationship difficulty and unusual health problems, you may want to reach out to a professional counselor or a physician to explore root causes.

My marital struggles played on an endless loop in my brain. Thinking about the future of my marriage sent me into despair. The thought of the family unit breaking up was on my mind day and night. The weight was heavy. It was excruciating to contemplate divorce, especially since my kids were so young. I'd never envisioned this reality for them. What I was contemplating was beyond devastating and made me feel as if I were dwelling at rock bottom.

One day during my lunch break, I went to the In-N-Out Burger drive-through. While in line, I burst into tears. I started talking toward the heavens. "Please, help me. Please. Please, help me." I physically directed my words toward the sky. I was overcome with hopelessness.

As I was driving away with my food, I heard a voice in my ear: "This is the hardest decision you've ever made." Startled, I looked around me. No one was there. After I caught my breath, I thought, *Oh my God. Thank you, Universe, for acknowledging my pain. Yes, this is the hardest decision I've ever made.*

I felt a sense of relief wash over me. I felt that someone was helping me, watching over me, affirming me. While the voice didn't point the way forward, the simple reassuring words were immensely comforting.

Shortly after, I had another odd experience. During a family trip to Scotland, we spent time at my aunt and uncle's house. While we were there, my uncle was suddenly struck with an incessant and painful toothache. Upon our return from the trip, my uncle was diagnosed with throat cancer. Sadly, he passed away a month later. He was someone I deeply respected.

Back in my dark bedroom one night, I saw a holographic image of him, wearing his usual crew sweater and khakis, standing across the room. My heart started beating quickly. *Are my eyes deceiving me?* I thought. I looked at him, and he just looked back at me with a big grin. After taking some deep breaths to calm myself, I took this vision to mean all was well; he had my back during this difficult time.

The exact same thing happened a few nights later. Yes, it did freak me out, but I said to myself, *Okay, Kate, stay calm. I choose to believe this is a sign and he's assuring me everything will be okay.*

The kids were young, my marriage was unraveling, and it hurt deeply. Despite our ongoing attempts to try to understand each other, my husband and I just couldn't get in sync. The relationship just couldn't be repaired. Times were extraordinarily difficult given that we had two toddlers running around needing all the attention. We were happy to provide them with it, though. They were joyful lights in a dark period.

My gut and my heart knew that the marital dynamic couldn't continue. The heartache and sadness were too much to endure. I also felt like my identity was coined as "pain in the ass." I was a smart woman becoming more in tune with reality. I was starting to see that the behavior directed toward me wasn't changing for the better—and that perhaps I wasn't exaggerating the extent of the problems after all.

17: DISSOLUTION

One evening, my mom came into town to watch the boys. She said that she wanted to offer us a much-deserved short break and send us out to dinner together.

The time had come for me. On this night, I'd need to enact the experiment I'd been thinking about. I made strict rules for myself. My intention was to gauge whether I was interpreting Tom's behavior correctly. Was he initiating arguments, unprovoked by me, then blaming me? I believed that I was being gaslit and needed to get a handle on it. Truly, how could communication and cooperation be impossible? It just didn't make logical sense.

And so, at dinner, I wouldn't initiate conversation. I'd sit there and respond politely and neutrally to everything. I'd nod, smile, and be agreeable.

We went to a cute Italian hole-in-the-wall. It could have been such a cozy, romantic evening—an opportunity to exhale and reconnect. I had to concentrate deeply to make sure I didn't veer away from my experiment. Smile. Nod. Speak in short, affirmative sentences. I've never been more strategically focused during an interaction. It was challenging to stay the course, but I did. And unfortunately, my experiment proved my hypothesis.

I didn't say much that evening, yet I was still pleasant and engaging. Despite that, I could see him working hard to spark an argument, spark chaos, spark drama. He was picking at me. I could see it as plain as day.

The results were devastating and dark. I was his wife. His partner of over a decade. We had kids together. Was I so horrible? Was I so unlikable? What was it?

Our dynamic was a situation that one can't make sense of unless they were part of it. I felt confused, abused, and gaslit, as I mentioned. I'm not diagnosing or assigning terms to what I experienced; rather, I'm suggesting that it's important to educate ourselves about behaviors directed toward us—and to not diagnose ourselves as the problem.

We drove home in silence. When we pulled into the driveway, the kids ran out to greet us. Fighting back the tears in my eyes, I made my way upstairs and offered my mom a cheerful thanks for watching the kids. I told her that we'd had a really nice time.

***

Months after that dinner with my husband, my youngest son graduated from his preschool on a beautiful May day at a park near our home. It was only a preschool graduation, but these preschool years had been challenging in so many ways. This felt like a celebratory occasion. My mom drove an hour and a half to celebrate this milestone with us.

After the event, we were all supposed to head back to our house and have lunch as a family. Instead, my husband got angry with me for something, and an argument ensued. Go figure. Arguments upset me and made me shut down emotionally—and who wants to spend time with someone who's upset? What a fantastic hall pass. He left the house to catch a golf tee time with friends. Victory for him.

At the party that followed the ceremony, I cried in front of my mom out of embarrassment and shame. It was a moment of reckoning for me.

I dug deep to find courage. I needed to share my truth and reality with my mom. I needed to confide in her about the dark events that had been happening in my life. And I did.

During that conversation, I divulged financial problems that I'd kept strictly to myself because I was ashamed. I was unaware that unpaid bills to a significant creditor had stacked up. I found this out by chance, when checking my credit report. The money issues staring me in the face were overwhelming. Possibly insurmountable. Despite trying to team up and get back on track, that did not seem to be the mutually agreeable plan.

The lies and deception entangled in the financial situation became my strongest motivator to end the marriage. The signs were directing me to focus on the bigger picture. I was being forced to protect myself emotionally and financially. The situation was another example of lack of transparency and misaligned priorities.

Tom didn't seem to have any kind of methodology to his work, schedule, or boundaries. Calls would come in at various times—days, nights, and weekends. I offered sympathy and grace for his seemingly challenging, around-the-clock work situation. I was convinced that his work was extremely demanding and more difficult than I could understand. I took him at his word when he said he was busting his ass, and I assumed that his earnings were commensurate with that.

During the eight years that we dated, my husband and I kept our finances separate. We had separate bank accounts. We split everything fifty-fifty, regardless of employment status or earnings.

When I was on a leave of absence after giving birth, and receiving a portion of my salary, I paid for my share of everything. I also paid for all baby expenditures. I was a team player. Taking care of things as a responsible person. A different structure wasn't discussed.

The mentality of "everything will just work itself out" is naive and foolish. Things don't just work themselves out. In a committed relationship, decisions and transparency are required. You need to decide what values are important to you. What processes and protocols are important to you. Conversations about these things can be difficult when you have an unwilling or uncooperative partner. It's important to be aware of behaviors that might not align with your values or desires, especially in the earliest parts of your relationship. Keep your eyes open.

You need to know who you are and what's important to you. If you're having difficulty identifying what values or behaviors are important to you, find a therapist, a coach, or a book to help you. If you don't live a life that's aligned with what's important to you, you might need to be ready to be disappointed. During our relationship, I never opened Tom's mail or requested access to his financial accounts. I was tipped off to his earnings only when I saw them listed on a tax form, when we began filing taxes jointly as a married couple with children. This tax form told me that during the time he was working around the clock, my earnings were double what he made. I was floored. I felt duped. Misled.

I was foolish because I was living in the land of assumptions. Having young children who demanded my attention dulled my interest in marital-business conversations. I was mentally exhausted. I used the excuse of being busy with young children as a reason to bury my head in the sand and assume financial matters would work themselves out. Until they didn't.

Ask your partner for a conversation, especially if it seems there's an issue to resolve. Trust your gut. Try to turn down the emotion and approach the conversation with facts. State your needs. If your partner is unwilling to have a conversation, I encourage you to seek professional help.

***

During the difficult months contemplating the future of my marriage, I decided to seek out a life coach with whom I could talk and find solace and resolutions. I hired someone who'd previously been a divorce attorney and was now coaching on relationships. I got a package of four phone calls. I'd book an appointment at a time when my husband was home and could watch the kids. Then I could step away and get into my car to have privacy for an hour. I'd drive a few blocks from my house, pull over, and park the car.

During my first three sessions, I was in full victim mode—explaining, rehashing, stressing, fretting. Not getting anywhere in particular. The sessions were cathartic to a degree, with crying always coming next, reflecting the depths of my agony.

What broke me so deeply was the thought of the breakup of the family unit. That heartbreak was at the core of my emotions.

During call number four, I was in the same vicious loop of analyzing, crying, and not getting anywhere. On that call, I went into full-blown hysterics. My coach could barely calm me. I couldn't help myself. I felt desperately hopeless, sitting there in the parked car, my sunglasses shielding my puffy and dripping eyes.

Finally, my coach yelled, "KATE, STOP. PLEASE TELL ME: WHAT DO YOU WANT?"

That did it. That stopped me in my tracks. What did I want? I sat in silence for a few minutes and deeply reflected.

Finally, I had a moment of clarity. "I want peace." I paused. "I want peace."

I felt at ease for a moment. I felt a way forward. I felt as if a weight had lifted from my body. I felt a glimmer of hope. I knew what my decision needed to be. I wanted peace. I needed peace. I could no longer live in the never-ending loop of despair and sadness.

At that moment, I decided that I'd go about implementing the very difficult decisions that would lead to reclaiming my peace.

What do you want in your life? What are your needs and values? What makes you happy? It's okay to claim this. You don't have to turn your life upside down overnight to attain it. Taking one small step toward your happiness will begin to create positive momentum.

Shortly after that coaching call, Tom and I agreed that we'd separate as amicably as possible. Kids first. Decisions were made. Actions would be implemented. Hearts were broken. New chapters would be written.

18: THE DIVORCE

I hired a divorce attorney in San Francisco, which meant I had to drive west over the Bay Bridge to meet at the attorney's office for the initial consultation. On this day, when I got to the San Francisco side of the bridge, I went from calm to breaking down. I was experiencing deep, profound sadness at what was about to happen to my children. Intense pain washed over me. Everything I'd never wanted but now needed on behalf of my health at every level was about to become real.

I was making the official move to end the marriage, which meant the kids would be from a "broken home." New, difficult chapters would become their reality.

I put on my sunglasses so nobody could see my tearful eyes and puffy face and then walked into the building on a busy street in Union Square. I soon realized that my attorney worked in the same building as a Ford Modeling Agency. As I was getting into the elevator, I was joined by a couple of gorgeous, fresh-faced young women. Stunning models. I wasn't sure if I should laugh or just keep crying. Life seemed so simple for these young, beautiful women with their lives and new decisions ahead of them.

I began the paperwork with my attorney, sharing details about why I was filing for divorce. After listening quietly and intently, she said that the situation sounded oppressive. I hadn't used that word before, but it described my situation accurately. I felt validated and appreciative that a third party could see that my reality had been difficult. That validation alone was probably worth the thousands of dollars that I spent to get the divorce proceedings started.

After only two months, though, I let her go. Working with an attorney was getting too costly. Next, I hired a mediator who required that both parties contribute financially to the process, and we were able to negotiate the most important details. The dissolution process took patience and perseverance.

Finally, I hired a do-it-yourself paperwork-filing company. They couldn't provide legal advice, but they could help us compile and file the right paperwork. After many months of our paperwork remaining stagnant, Tom agreed to move forward and meet at their offices to get it done. Our tense body language spoke volumes to them. Bless those workers who helped us that day.

Two years after I started the process, the divorce was final.

***

My kids were my universe. Because of that, I made a commitment to myself: if divorce was imminent, I'd do everything in my power to maintain a friendly, productive relationship with the father of my children, so we could coparent harmoniously.

After Tom and I separated and before we officially divorced, we tried to come together as a unit for dinners or short outings. It felt like the right thing to do. It also felt overly challenging and inauthentic. The relationship was strained and difficult.

You might have heard about the concept of conscious uncoupling, and that was my intention. Divorce impacts children. Respectful and cooperative coparenting relationships are optimal. I know many former couples who are friends, friendly, or perfectly civil toward one another. Every individual will adopt a different coparenting style—it's about what works best for them and their family.

I advocate for every individual being treated respectfully. If you don't like the way you're being treated in a coparenting relationship, or you don't like the way you feel, be honest with yourself. Sometimes, removing yourself from interactions with a coparent is a choice you need to make for self-preservation and protection. Sometimes blocking someone's phone number and removing yourself entirely is a self-honoring option to consider. Seek professional help and other resources to navigate increasingly difficult circumstances.

Post-divorce, I was feeling worn down and emotionally exhausted. I needed professional support, someone with whom I could talk to about the difficulties of coparenting. I turned to my company's employee assistance program to find a counselor and began a series of supportive and helpful conversations.

My new therapist loaned me a book about alcoholism and codependency. I was confused. Once again, I didn't think books on these topics pertained to me.

This therapist told me that I was acting in codependent ways, but I didn't believe this to be true. Frankly, I didn't understand the concept of codependency in the context of my situation. The dots weren't connecting for me.

More than ever, I believe that we need accessible educational programs that help people understand addiction and codependency in terms of behaviors and implications. With information and comprehension, we're empowered to make better choices for ourselves.

My therapist was very supportive of the steep challenges that I faced in coparenting. After just a couple of weeks of our working together, she asked me if I felt as if I needed to take stronger measures to advocate for myself and the children.

I was extremely frustrated and just trying to cope—but her question brought my mind to a screeching halt. The question was crucial. A different plan was in fact needed.

We can't always see things for ourselves. Professional support can help us move forward on our path in a healthy way. I was just trying to soldier on as a coparent, trying my hardest to dismiss and suppress my feelings about behaviors and antics aimed at me. Thankfully, instead of simply listening to me week after week and nodding, my therapist was an active thought partner.

In working to heal and move beyond the challenges, I've done a great deal of research on many topics related to my inner-child wounds and patterns. I've also researched and studied personality disorders and further explored why I'm attracted to the type of people I'm attracted to.

I once had a boss urge me to never diagnose someone. I came to understand that unless someone has received a clinical diagnosis, we can never be sure what's "wrong," and it's unfair to assign a diagnosis. As previously mentioned, there is terminology that I feel applies to my situation.

I encourage you to educate yourself and devise a plan regarding how you might navigate the dynamics or behaviors impacting your life.

19: PHOENIX RISING

To earn extra income during my separation and divorce transition, I put on an entrepreneurial hat. I was working for a sports organization that had a ready-to-run youth tennis program, and they needed more providers. Though I'd made a career in human resources, I'd also been a tennis player. *Why not run a program like this?* I thought. *Why not make a positive impact working with youth?*

I took steps to launch the after-school tennis program at two elementary schools in my area and helped meet a growing need at these schools. I had fun running this program, and it was also an excellent source of supplemental income that helped me bridge the financial gap before I returned to a full-time corporate job.

In this tennis-teaching role, I needed assistance in each class with the twenty high-energy elementary school kids. A colleague introduced me to a local retiree, a former doctor, who loved tennis, was a jovial spirit, and was grateful to be a helping hand in this program. He'd typically help me on Fridays.

Friday afternoons always seemed to be the time when Tom and I had overly emotional discussions on the phone. We were in divorce proceedings and learning how to be a two-house family. Additionally, my nerves would be tender by the end of the week as I juggled everything. Sometimes I'd come to the Friday program with my eyes a little puffy from crying.

Coach, as I called my colleague, could read my body language in an instant. "Hey, are you okay?" he'd ask. Though part of me was ashamed that I wasn't projecting a "having it all together" vibe, I trusted Coach and shared quite a bit with him about my personal challenges. He knew I was in the thick of struggles with my ex and getting myself stable as a newly single mom. His caring approach toward me meant a lot during our year and a half running this program. I certainly received as much from Coach as the kids did. After our great run, I concluded the program—it was time for me to shift back into a full-time corporate job with higher compensation and generous benefits to support my family.

Multiple income streams can be a beautiful thing. My "side hustle" enabled me to put a large chunk of money in my bank account, which helped me through a time of transition. What I wanted next was corporate safety—which, by the way, is a myth. But at that time, a corporate nine-to-five at an exciting, global company with career growth opportunity felt right for my family and me.

When I accepted this job, as a single parent, I knew that I would need help with my boys. My new job was going to be demanding, with both a commute and travel required. My parents became Earth angels with my boys. They went above and beyond in every way. Not only were they helping, but a deeper bond also was formed between all of us. Grandma and Grandpa truly became "the village"—and we all benefited. My boys would not be who they are today without my parents' positive influence and love for them. The word *grateful* can't even begin to express my feelings.

***

Navigating the separation and divorce was mentally trying for so many reasons. Growing my career was a great avenue for compartmentalizing the pain. I tried to keep my personal issues out of the workplace. A few people knew bits and pieces about my personal life, but mostly I focused on the work at hand and created a happy day for myself.

You might feel as if you're holding it all together (emotionally, physically, spiritually), but your body can tell a different story. I now realize that my body and mind could (and would) exude how I felt on the inside.

***

I moved to a new community after the marital separation. Joining a new community and placing my kids in a new school felt overwhelming but also gave me hope. All I wanted was for my kids to fit into their new school and community. Thankfully, a couple of weeks after my younger son started first grade, he made new friends. I was volunteering in the classroom and got my first look at all the kids—they played together, laughed, and followed each other around the room. I was relieved and giddy.

I walked up to the mom of one of these boys with a smile and said, "It looks like our boys are friends and having fun together!" She gave me a curt, somewhat patronizing smile and walked away.

Welcome to the neighborhood! It seemed that parental friendships in this community had been formed and locked in in nursery school. I guess I'd missed the window for joining the inner circle. Despite the frost from some, I still volunteered in the classrooms and showed up with a smile. My son made many friends. Kind and inclusive parents were out there.

No matter the day or custody schedule, I'd attend most of my kids' sporting and extracurricular activities. Even if they weren't coming home with me that day, we'd see each other and talk, which made me feel better.

As the days and weeks passed, I began to rise like a phoenix. Slow and steady.

I didn't want a dime from the inevitable sale of our marital house. Freedom has no price. I remember coming home from work one day after being in my post-marriage rental house for a month. I sat down in a chair that faced the fireplace, which exuded warmth and created a calm atmosphere. I exhaled fully. I felt peaceful. There was nobody around to antagonize me. I could just be. How great it is to just *be*. I even bought a doormat that said *Peace*. I was claiming it.

Some people won't like it when you're happy. They might even try to convince you that you're not happy. But there's no point in trying to convince someone of your happiness, especially if they don't have your best interests at heart. Feel your feelings and claim your feelings. This might seem obvious, but it's a bizarre dynamic when someone is trying to control you by way of telling you how you feel. Surround yourself with people who exude good energy and lift you up. Even if that means listening to an inspirational podcast. Break the chains and enjoy the good feelings.

It took me a few years to recover from my anger and victim mentality about being the primary financial provider in my marriage and for my children post-marriage. As I started making more money in my career, I knew that I was blessed to be earning more and no longer struggling financially. I knew it would be best for my overall health to begin releasing my anger. I started paying for everything with an attitude of gratitude. The situation just was. I was facing reality.

Meanwhile, my dad would rant about the ongoing lack of "shared" responsibility, attempting to rally for justice. I had to help him understand that "fair" just wasn't going to happen. Fair is where you go to find the merry-go-round and the clowns.

At times in my marriage, especially after we had kids, I'd take on masculine, driving energy to get life's business taken care of. My instinct simply told me to take charge and execute—pay the thing, buy the thing, book the thing. If someone else wasn't going to step in and step up to provide for the household, I would. This type of behavior could certainly emasculate a partner. It could also let someone off the hook, which they might secretly want. Tom never seemed emasculated, but I now understand how my instinct to take over perhaps created a recipe for resentment (on both sides).

There's no right or wrong when it comes to how to lead a relationship and family and who earns the money. It's about mutual agreement. I fantasized about my partner supporting the household financially. Fantasized? Why didn't I articulate this and share my desires with him?

We can't thrive in an environment of poor communication and lack of mutual understanding. Assumptions are dangerous. Taking a path of least resistance and avoiding agreements is foolish.

1

2

3

4

5

6

20: TRUE LOVE

It's only in the last couple of years, having reflected deeply on my childhood experiences, that I've come to comprehend that my belief that *you stay in relationships at any cost* was deeply wired in. Completely normal. I used this approach in most of my relationships—romantic and platonic. It's no surprise that once I liked a romantic partner, I'd dig in and stay at any cost, despite seeing yellow or red flags. I was willing to bend and go with the flow, ignoring my intuition. All for one and one for all.

I was a team player and loyal. I had a deep desire to be liked—my primary school belief about not being desired ran deep. What I didn't realize was that these behaviors were signs that I felt unworthy. Often in romantic relationships, I felt as if I might not be able to do any better. This was as good as it could get. I would stay and trust that *they* would do better.

Better relationships? Did they exist? Yes, there's a whole world full of millions of incredible humans out there.

I forgive myself for these misunderstandings. I didn't know about possibility, grace, and learning to feel worthy of receiving an upgrade. I release the judgment and lack of awareness.

I've changed my internal dialogue so that it conjures up better feelings. I now tell myself: *I'm worthy of being in relationships where people treat me with respect, integrity, consistency, kindness, honesty, and generosity. I'm worthy of people who desire to bring their best selves to the relationship.*

In the current chapter of my life, I practice trusting that people give me their best because these are the people that I'm becoming a magnet for. My affirmations continue to express that I attract people who care and act with high levels of integrity. I must trust that I attract and draw in people with the highest of positive intentions. I'm grateful when we find each other.

Here's an affirmation I like to use to get myself into a higher vibration: *I interact with people who want to support me and treat me with positive regard. High honor, high care, high love, high integrity, high vibe, high consistency, high deliverables. My bar is high. Their bar is high. Together, we're on the same level.*

"The better it gets, the better it gets."[9]

If you're not attracting new relationships at a higher level, give it time. Your energetic vibration is rising, and it may take time for your physical mind and body to follow. Hold on. I share this from experience.

I hope that my stories inspire people to pause and reflect carefully. Then, I hope they pass the book on to someone else with whom these messages might resonate. Let's empower and support each other as we make big decisions and explore new paths.

***

After the divorce was finalized, Tom and I still had to communicate regarding the children. Conversations were rarely productive. There came a time when I started requesting an agenda for our phone conversations, so we could get straight to the important topics and simply cross them off one by one. The interactions were still tense, though, and the old ways of conversing didn't serve me. He wasn't interested in my ideas or solutions. Perhaps it seemed to him as though I were trying to control him by proposing solutions.

I needed to try new ways of establishing boundaries.

After one particularly difficult and demeaning conversation, I was done. I was moving forward with my life, and the old ways were over. I would no longer engage like this. I decided that I'd never take another phone call from him. And I didn't.

I suggested that we email each other if there was something to communicate. Email would also provide a paper trail. He kept calling and texting me. Months later, he realized I wouldn't pick up the phone.

Not picking up the phone was an important milestone in my healing journey. It might sound counterproductive or punitive. Quite the opposite—it allowed me to take back my personal power. Boundaries. Something new to me. I was consciously taking charge of how someone spoke to me and how I was treated. This new approach absolutely helped preserve my health. Unfortunately, there was an unintended consequence. My kids, who were getting older and more independent, became the middlemen.

My not speaking to their dad was necessary for my self-preservation. This decision wasn't made lightly. It was severe. I felt I had no other choice. As I mentioned, productive coparenting is ideal. Strive for it. Try everything you can on behalf of the children. Consult with professionals. Ultimately, you must protect your peace.

Cue the next life milestone. Due to a circumstance in my ex's living situation, my children came to live with me full time and there was no more coparenting. It was just me. This new dynamic positively impacted me physically, emotionally, and spiritually. The oppression and chaos lifted. I was left alone. This created significant peace and ease.

***

Having children is a massive blessing and one of the most challenging undertakings one can imagine. I've given my all to my children.

I've reflected on why I'm here on Earth. What's my purpose? What's my calling? While I've always known how important my children are, when I ask the Universe that big question, the answer comes back more clearly than ever.

I'm here on Earth to be a mom to my two boys. Why am I here? For them. My love for them is the truest love I'll ever know.

As I was going through the emotional difficulty of my divorce and the aftermath, the days could be long and dark. My children always brightened my day. Always.

On an episode of *The Oprah Winfrey Show*, author Toni Morrison posed a question: "When a kid walks in the room, your child . . . does your face light up?"[10] For me, the answer is a resounding yes. No matter how exhausted or worn out I felt during those tumultuous years, my heart and soul always felt so blessed and grateful to be their mom.

My boys and I have been the Three Musketeers for many years. The three of us never argue or even bicker. We're a tight, cooperative unit. We all behave respectfully toward each other. We're considerate. We legitimately like each other. We get each other.

Intentionally, due to lessons learned from my childhood, I run a house with very little drama. The tone and temperature are always even-keeled at my house. I run a tight, positive ship.

Now and again, I reflect on the early, demanding days of solo parenting. Depletion. Juggling. Working. Driving. Volunteering. Battling. Meeting. Financing. Cooking. Chaperoning. Nurturing. Cheering. Hoping. Helping. Monitoring. I was there.

The tunnel could be dark and bleak. There were days, weeks, and years when it felt as if the grind, the routines, and the struggles would never end. I just got up and did it again, and again, and again. Not complaining. Remaining calm.

The Three Musketeers' daily routines "broke up" when my oldest son went to college. His departure felt surreal and sad, but my son assured me that all was well; he would be okay. He was now the one providing emotional support to me, and I was proud of him. I knew that his college journey had come at just the right time for him.

The morning after dropping him off at college, I felt a bit numb. Then, as I stared out of a window, a giant wave of emotion washed over my body, and my eyes welled up with tears. I cried. For about an hour. The emotion wasn't sadness. It was actually victory. Victory.

I analyzed my tears. They were tears of joy. Tears of immense pride. It was a steep mountain. My sons and I are summiting it. Our path ahead is bright.

REFLECTIONS ON LOVE

Below are journal-writing prompts that refer to themes I've shared in Part 2. There's no need to reflect on all of them. Choose one or a few. If you find the prompts helpful, come back and answer more. Sometimes focusing on one or two ideas at a time can help build momentum. Get curious about any insights that come up and seek professional counseling or find a coach if you need deeper support.

Suggested journal-writing prompts:

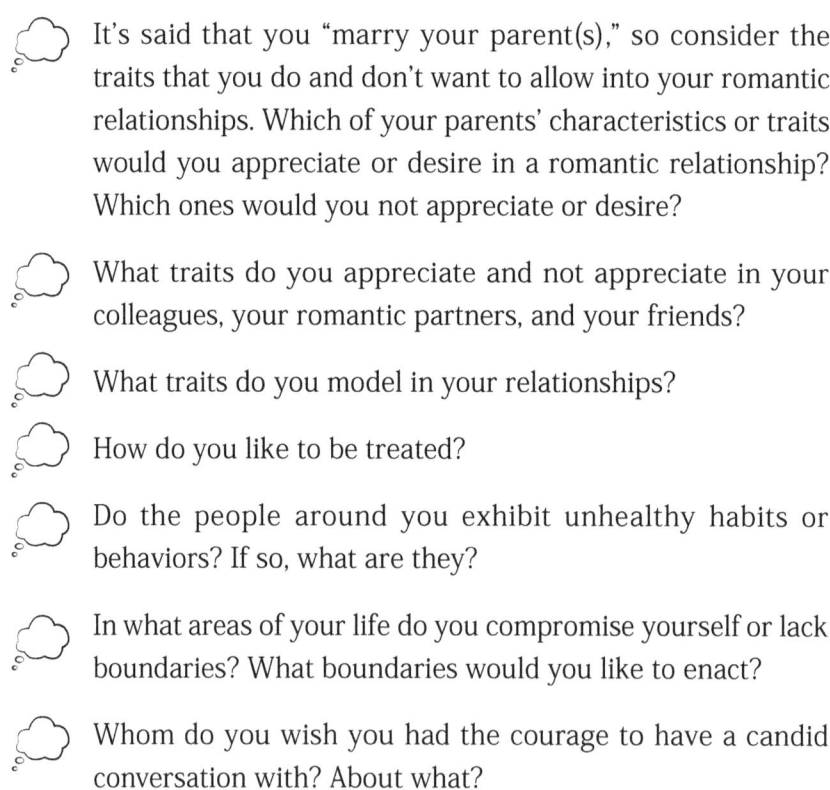

- It's said that you "marry your parent(s)," so consider the traits that you do and don't want to allow into your romantic relationships. Which of your parents' characteristics or traits would you appreciate or desire in a romantic relationship? Which ones would you not appreciate or desire?

- What traits do you appreciate and not appreciate in your colleagues, your romantic partners, and your friends?

- What traits do you model in your relationships?

- How do you like to be treated?

- Do the people around you exhibit unhealthy habits or behaviors? If so, what are they?

- In what areas of your life do you compromise yourself or lack boundaries? What boundaries would you like to enact?

- Whom do you wish you had the courage to have a candid conversation with? About what?

As I reflect on "Love," here are some of my key takeaways. I encourage you to contemplate these actions or consider making your own list.

Actions to help you strengthen your sense of self-worth:

1. Identify the desires and values that you hold most closely. Audit your relationships and determine if your needs are being met.

2. Determine where you draw your line in the sand regarding your needs, wants, desires, values, goals, and vision. Stay true to yourself.

3. Clearly and kindly articulate your needs in a relationship, despite the potential outcome.

4. Be honest with yourself and identify if addiction or substance abuse—even the usage seems social—is part of the relationship and if the outcome of that behavior matches your needs and desires.

5. Remind yourself that we teach people how to treat us (and remember, people will show you who they are—believe them).

6. If you're on the receiving end of antagonistic behavior, or if you simply don't like the way your partner is treating you, seek professional help and be extremely specific about what you're experiencing. Your concerns are legitimate.

7. Don't give your power away by deferring your wants and needs.

8. If you're entering a committed relationship, establish agreements, financial and otherwise. Who pays for what? Don't act hastily and wing it.

Concepts to remember when you're doubting yourself and need to activate self-trust:

- If something doesn't feel right, seem right, or look right, trust your gut—because your gut is right.
- What you want and need in a relationship might evolve as the years go by. Be honest about it. Be gentle with and honor yourself when making difficult decisions.
- You can't change people. But you can change yourself.
- Teamwork doesn't always make the dream work in a relationship.
- You can't play all the positions on the field in a relationship.
- Seek professional help but leave if you need to. Trust yourself to do so.

Anything can be changed, fixed, or improved. At any age.

PART 3: LEADERSHIP

*"I choose me. I choose myself. I choose my kids
and family and business and future. I choose
how we do things. I choose who I am and how
I show up. I choose the life I want. I choose
healing and growth and goodness."*

–Amanda Frances[11]

In this book, I've shared some stories that might make me sound like a victim. I've never thought of myself this way or wanted to embrace that mentality. I have been in the depths of chaos and despair and felt unable to find my way out, despite my best efforts. Still, all my experiences made me stronger, provided reflection points, and helped me grow.

Becoming a leader in your own life can involve a lot of reflection and intentional decisions, but personal power is priceless. Life has taught me many lessons that paved the way toward greater self-awareness, which fuels what I refer to as "self-leadership"—making empowering and thoughtful decisions on behalf of myself. I now want to share the leadership concepts and mindset tools that in recent years have helped me rebuild my life and make more intentional, life-affirming decisions. I want to share how I stopped surviving and started thriving.

The life-redesign tools that I've used include both practical actions and spiritual concepts. As a career professional and mom to two boys, I've been able to work with these tools—I won't be sharing anything that I haven't personally tried and benefited from. I continue to mix and match my tools (sometimes multiple times a day), as certain aspects of my life are a work in progress.

I'm one of the least patient people I know. I like to focus on something and get a result quickly. Some of these tools allow for this, and others require results to simmer on the stove before they boil, so to speak. I might not see a result within days, but months later, I might have an aha moment and think, *Okay, interesting, I can see the shift today!*

Changes don't happen with the snap of a finger. At least they don't for me. It takes planning, intention, and commitment to make things happen. It requires tenacity and determination. If something is important enough to me, it will get done.

I initially decided to write this next section solely about my career—and share business learnings. I've done a lot of analysis during the book writing process and realized more distinctly that I've had to enact a lot of self-awareness and behaviors that initiated *leadership advice* on behalf of myself. So, this section speaks to a more wholistic conversation about career, decision-making, and leadership tools in my life.

21: LEADERSHIP STYLES

As the first-born kid, I told my younger brother what to do when we were growing up. It felt natural. I was both his protector and his guide. My family called me bossy. I don't object to that. I embodied confidence in my household and neighborhood.

I enjoyed organizing, participating, and refereeing our neighborhood sports games. I was only one or two years older than the other kids but felt much older—and wiser. Nobody told me that I was wiser. It was all self-appointed leadership. As mentioned, it was school social dynamics that made me start questioning myself. My self-esteem and confidence would get dismantled in this setting.

Competitive tennis was a much-needed confidence booster. My individual leadership skills were absolutely required on the court playing singles. Nobody was there to rescue me. Coaching from the sidelines wasn't allowed, so I had to fend for myself with every decision. This helped improve my decision-making skills and taught me to maintain my composure during difficult or unfair matches.

Entering my business career, I didn't come out swinging as a leader. I was in observation mode. As I shared, in the earliest days of my career, I believed that I had to pay my dues before I could more confidently use my voice at work.

I'm grateful that, when I was in my teens, my mom told me that I could do anything. I heard her. In those days, my mom seemed to believe that my dreams would be possible mostly by way of a successful tennis career. When my competitive tennis career ended, I felt as if I'd abandoned success. Thankfully, I was wrong.

***

In the nineties, while working at my first HR job, I came across a magazine article about life coaching. As a speech communication major and a new HR professional, I felt that life coaching sounded like a dream job. I had to know more.

I explored the program material that explained the training and was hooked. I decided to invest in a coaching certification program. The live training was delivered by tele-calls, and the material was presented via CD-ROM. During the class, I'd lie on my bedroom floor holding my landline phone to my ear with one hand and taking notes with the other. (Ah, how far we've come with technology.)

I enjoyed these classes. As the courses progressed, we were required to conduct live coaching with a fellow student, as practice. We'd be critiqued on our coaching by the instructor and our classmates. And that's when impostor syndrome struck. Who was I, in my twenties, to be life-coaching someone? Could I legitimately offer value?

Despite my enthusiasm for the concept of life coaching, I also began to wonder if it was corny or even fraudulent. What I didn't fully comprehend back then was that life coaches are the guide, not the problem-solver. I mistakenly believed that my fifteen-minute coaching-practice sessions needed to solve someone's issue. The self-inflicted pressure to show up perfectly felt intense. I should have consulted with the instructors. Instead, I stopped going to class.

I designated this decision as a personal failure.

However, I integrated and applied the coaching skills I learned in the program to my HR career. I'd had it all wrong. Throughout my career, I came to learn that HR is practically 99 percent coaching conversations. Having both provided and received life coaching, I can say it's one of the most helpful jobs on the planet.

Think about it: Professional athletes and Olympians have coaches. Executives have coaches. Why isn't everyone else who has a dream, a goal, or a dilemma deserving of a coach? You are. Hire one. Who knows, maybe your boss will invest in you and pay for it.

I'm proud of my twenty-something self for hearing and answering the call of coaching. On reflection, I can see that sometimes we follow an intuitive calling or interest that pays off in ways that won't present themselves until later. Your interests and aspirations—whether unproven or unpopular, or not trendy—can always be pursued and become a clue as to the special gifts you can bring to the world.

***

I've shared that many of my mentors were the inspirational leaders I found in books and on TV. These important mentors weren't people with whom I interacted in person. By way of their teaching, I learned just how big my desires could be, and that they were attainable. I also spent thousands of hours observing and taking part in business meetings where different leadership behaviors and styles played out. I read biographies and personal-development books to absorb as much external knowledge and know-how as possible. All this information shaped my own leadership style.

Over the years, I put together puzzle pieces regarding which leadership traits and attributes in a work setting that I liked and didn't like. At the top of the list of likes was being on the receiving end of a flexible management style. I appreciated the supportive, motivational bosses who inspired me. I liked being around managers who were able to exhibit humor, laugh, and even be a little self-deprecating. I watched leaders who could defuse challenging meetings, lower people's stress, and create positive outcomes. I also appreciated those who were organized and on time and who thoughtfully helped me understand the performance targets that we were aiming for. Those who were available for conversations and offered a human touch were extra extraordinary.

As a senior leader, I'm required to share my knowledge and point of view, and often to provide a directive. For me, *how* I share it is crucial. What's my tone and intent? I choose to lead with kindness and positive intention. Being kind also means being honest. I find that being honest and forthright saves time because you don't dance around the issues.

It's not that people don't ever frustrate me. They do. But my experience allows me greater perspective and patience. When I extend kindness and professionalism, I feel as if I'm living in integrity, regardless of others' responses.

In the early years of my life, I felt as if playing the role of the Bitch gave me a sense of power. As I got my career going, I realized that I liked to show up with kindness. It felt better.

Through my business, I teach and pass along my knowledge to help others grow and get better at their jobs and pursuits. I help remove roadblocks. I lead with empathy and flexibility. I engage in conversation and ask for opinions. I like to be motivating, encouraging, curious. I drive for results, adding humor and laughter wherever possible, reading the room. I bring positivity, I help to uncomplicate matters, and I don't desire a spotlight—I'd rather shine the spotlight on others. Some people have advised that I be "more boisterous" and step into a bolder spotlight, but that doesn't feel natural to me. I choose when to be outspoken, knowing when and where I add value.

On my life and leadership journey, I've learned that people want to be seen and heard. That's the way I want them to feel when they talk to me or work with me. I'm also not afraid of silence in a conversation. When there's silence, it's important for one or both of us to collect and process our thoughts and not rush or force a response. I like to make sure that I offer thoughtful responses, and sometimes that requires a long pause beforehand. I like to empower my teams, my clients, and even my kids by speaking respectfully and thoughtfully. Building trust is key.

In my line of work, I aim to coach people toward attaining their desired results. It's about supporting people to do their best. There may be misses or failures (both mine and theirs). Failure used to scare me. I'm growing to get over that. It's not easy to watch someone fall short, but sometimes our failures are our best lessons.

***

No two individuals are cut from the same mold. Each of us is unique, and each of us has our own strengths and capabilities. It's about identifying your strengths and leveraging them. I teach a Masterclass called "The #1 Fix to Transform Your Career." In this training, the focus is on seeking feedback as a business professional. Feedback is gold.

Feedback can help you identify the fastest way to strengthen your impact and improve your results. It can also help you become more aware of your desires. It helps create cohesion and connection between you and those that work with or for you. Additionally, it can get people excited to work with or for you toward your goals. Helping companies build and launch feedback loops (360-degree reviews; 360-degree debriefs and coaching) is one of my favorite services. Feedback can seem scary, but when provided in a container that feels safe and supportive, it's a surprising game changer.

Again, listening carefully and thoughtfully, with the aim of under-standing an individual's journey, is a critical part of my work as a coach and consultant. As humans, sometimes we're so eager to jump to provide a response, or to fill the air. But providing the space to let someone talk is one of the most powerful things we can do to support another person.

A trusted group of people who support and encourage you is priceless. The importance of coaching conversations is unmatched.

I recently took part in a coaching program where I received twenty-minute one-on-one coaching calls once per week. I brought one topic to each meeting and ended the call feeling heard, supported, and clear about what I would do next. One call even shifted my entire mindset as I headed into my weekend. I went from feeling overwhelmed to peaceful in twenty minutes. I believe that coaching conversations support a positive mindset and overall clarity.

There are many leadership styles and methods out there. For me, complex methodologies make no sense. Yes, we need principles, processes, and procedures. But they need not be complicated. For me, it's about operating with respect as a baseline. With curiosity about others, we can treat people in the ways that they want to be treated. Ask questions. You might be surprised by just how positively this can impact all your relationships.

22: WORK/LIFE

Life continues to offer me opportunities to reflect on, as well as new decisions that will support me.

It's inevitable that work and life blend together. Sometimes we bring a bad day at work home with us. Over time, as I became better at managing my mind, I felt like I could usually check work at the door.

Similarly, I kept most of my personal goings-on personal. When it came to my divorce, there were only a handful of people in corporate life that I would confide in. Work was often a respite from personal challenges. Even on days that felt heavy, I would show up to work with a good attitude and a smile.

Who knew that a business conversation would be a conduit to making an important personal realization and decision?

A few years into my expansive and busy corporate role at a major entertainment company, I had a meeting with the top executive, Mr. X. He worked in a different geographic location than I did. When he traveled to my office, he'd periodically schedule time to meet with me, the primary HR leader in the office. He was my boss's boss's boss—quite a bit up the chain from me. His executive assistant would contact me a week or two in advance to ask what my intended agenda was during this meeting. I'd reply expeditiously and let her know the three or four topics that I thought would be most important to discuss. Typically, I'd share relevant updates about the large corporate division with whom I worked closely and supported.

Mr. X seemed to appreciate my perspective during our meetings, and despite his status, he was easy to talk to. After I shared my updates, we'd sometimes veer into other business topics. I always made sure to ask questions and gain knowledge and insight from him where possible. I felt these conversations were important for me on many levels.

It was fascinating to observe how he carried himself. He was a media-trained executive, always on point. And so, it was important to me to follow suit and show up to our meetings organized and ready to engage in dialogue.

On this meeting day, Tom called me at the office. I was still taking calls from him at any time of the day at this point. I always felt obligated to answer, assuming he wanted to talk about something important involving our children. As often happened, the tone took a turn and the discussion became an argument. I couldn't keep talking. I ended the call about an hour prior to my important meeting. I knew that I needed to clear my mind and refresh myself on my notes one more time.

The interactions with Tom were so heavy and disheartening. It could sometimes feel as if I'd just participated in an obstacle course when I got off the phone with him, except I'd feel mentally drained.

Still, I was well versed in compartmentalizing my job duties and shaking things off.

Mr. X arrived right on time. In my office, we sat at my surfboard-shaped guest table and discussed the items on my agenda; the tone was always friendly and professional, and neither of us hesitated to punctuate the conversation with a little humor. About thirty minutes later (he was an expert time manager—one of the best I've encountered) our meeting wrapped up. I appreciated his time and the conversation.

A couple of days later, my boss called me. She wanted to ask me something, and I could sense slight trepidation. She finally asked, "How was your meeting with Mr. X?" I recapped some of the conversation and shared positive sentiments.

There was a pause. "Hmmm," she said. "That's interesting." She went on to kindly tell me that Mr. X felt I had not been prepared for the meeting and that I was off focus, or something to that effect.

I was surprised and disappointed by the feedback. I'd been prepared and on point. Or so I'd thought. As I reflected over the next few days, I came to wonder if the phone call with my ex had shaken me subconsciously and energetically, subsequently impacting my body language, demeanor, or focus. I needed to think about this more deeply.

What I came to realize was that despite my belief that I was performing well, my inner self had been affected by the challenging ongoing personal situation. The negative interactions with Tom, especially during the business day, were disrupting my peace and stability—apparently outwardly.

My body, my energy, was telling a story that I couldn't suppress. I felt disappointed with myself. I'd thought I was in the advanced league for compartmentalizing. Through this, I learned to embrace the fact that I'm a human being. I didn't end up telling my boss the backstory or these personal revelations. It didn't really matter anyway. The meeting had been what it had been.

What really mattered was the promise I made to myself as a result of this experience: I would never, *ever*, take another phone call from my ex-husband during my business day.

Just because someone familiar contacts you doesn't mean that you're obligated to engage. You may not realize that certain interactions impact your demeanor, no matter how good you are at compartmentalizing.

For context, this incident was my *first* "no more calls" boundary placed. Next, it was no phone calls at all.

It may seem harsh to place such boundaries, but these were important life assessment moments where I would no longer participate in conversations that didn't make me feel good. These were important realizations, milestones on my journey, that helped me take control of how I wanted to be treated.

23. BIG DECISIONS

I've shared stories about making big decisions. For me, each big decision was guided by inner knowing, new boundaries, research, dreams, goals—and digging deep to implement courage.

I'm going to be real: Life redesign isn't for the faint of heart. It's for the courageous, the bold. Change takes commitment and nerve. If I'm honest, it can feel scary. It takes a plan. Redesigning your life can be done in small increments. Or bigger increments. It's up to you.

Throughout the process, a pesky little gremlin likes to sit on our shoulders. It's called ego. Ego usually guides us toward the path of least resistance, which feels good. Comforting. The human ego is wired to keep us safe and protected. Ego tells us, "I just need one more certification before I feel qualified to start that project," or "Once my kids are older, I can leave my difficult marriage," or "I just need to save more money before I make that investment," or "I'll quit that job and pursue my other dreams in a year or two." The ego just goes on and on.

But the ego is the one that *thinks*, not the one that *does*. You have decision-making power, if you so choose. You can go against the thoughts produced by your ego. The life-redesign tools I'll share have helped me change my ego's default narrative. I can now tell myself: *Life evolves. Our needs change. Our desires change. Our likes change. We grow. We learn. We observe. We can welcome the new.*

When we're children, adults ask us what we want to be, and we might feel compelled to fill in the answer straightaway. Then, implement. Our life often becomes the result of a plan that we set years or even decades ago.

For me, it seemed like the proper life path involved going to college, getting married, and pursuing an incredible career. My sights were fairly basic in my early years. Peers of mine who'd grown up in wealthier communities or had direct access to mentors might have had more robust life-planning conversations. I was a middle-class kid with one parent who had substance abuse issues and one parent who'd left home at nineteen to become an au pair (my mom had guts). My parents never discussed goal planning nor life design with me. My dad had a degree from a prestigious college, and it hung in our spare bedroom. That was helpful to see. Mostly though, life seemed to involve navigating things one day at a time. I had ambition, but I felt as if things would unfold in due time.

My inner journey and life challenges ended up leading me to dig deep and rise to levels of resiliency that made me feel like a superhero at times. Failure wasn't an option; I couldn't reveal any cracks in my armor. As a single parent with a big career, I had to juggle multiple balls, and I set impossible standards for myself. Maintaining that kind of resiliency can put your mind and body into overdrive. For me, it wasn't a healthy place to be every day. Nonetheless, I operated in this mode for years. I trained my mind and body to persevere.

When I began my "midlife" intentional life redesign, my focus was on dissolving my marriage to reclaim peace and order in my life. Fast-forward years later to the middle of the global pandemic. I quit my well-paying job after two decades in corporate life. Why? I was ready for change. This was where my making big decisions got better, juicier, and more expansive for me. Never mind that I had to send a kid to college four months after I quit, or that I had other financial obligations.

By way of my broad and diverse human resources experience, I came to identify the business areas in which I loved working—and importantly, which areas weren't as interesting to me. In any job, there will likely be tasks and responsibilities that will feel tedious or outside of our zone of genius. That's okay. What's important is to consider (and perhaps journal about) why we like and dislike parts of our work. Doing so can help us make decisions that lead to more fulfilling destinations.

Over the years, I felt more energized when I was leading one-on-one coaching, small-group workplace conversations, and team-building. I enjoyed strategizing, analyzing, problem-solving, and getting to the actions that create better outcomes. For most of my career, I liked the structure and comfort of a corporate routine. Toward the end of it, I wanted greater freedom and flexibility around whom I worked with, what I worked on, and how and where I got my work done, as well as stewardship of my income. I decided that I wanted to be my own boss and work on my own terms. I wanted to launch my own business.

Based on my company's second-job policy and the overall optics, I knew that I'd need to resign before launching my business. I needed to be fully uncoupled. And so, I began planning my exit from the corporate world. My journey toward self-employment was multifaceted. It involved financial reviews, mindset work, visioning, goal setting, and more. The day I left my corporate job, I had zero clients. I had a general plan. And a boatload of trust in myself. I took inspiration from American essayist, John Burroughs's words, *I leaped, trusting that the net would appear.*[12]

I've always found exceptional community within my corporate jobs. This is where most of my like-minded people are. I appreciate my corporate colleagues' intelligence, kindness, humor, and more, and I've formed warm friendships inside the workplace. When I left, I knew that I needed to find new communities of like-minded people. So far, I've found a mixed bag of professional communities in the entrepreneurial world. I've looked to replicate the same high level of intelligent conversations, support, humor, and ambition around achieving goals.

I've found supportive individuals who taught me how to run an online business. I've met other individuals who were all too happy to invite me into their paid business communities and then underdelivered. I ended up feeling duped by their shiny marketing. Despite being new to certain aspects of business outside of the corporate world, I realize that I'm smarter and more capable than I often give myself credit for. Nonetheless, I'm still seeking high-level, high-vibe communities where I can learn, grow, and feel supported.

I've had days and moments of sheer panic on my new path: *When is my plan going to start getting some traction?* I've had days of elation. As the months have gone by, I've become more and more diligent with my mindset work. I do a *ton* of mindset work.

I now have an ever-growing HR consulting and executive-coaching business that leverages my years of business and HR experience. Plus, I have so many unique new business friends. Now that I work from home as an entrepreneur and my kids are older, life feels less hectic. I'm out of overdrive mode. It's often suggested that life is more intense when you're an entrepreneur, but this isn't true for me.

Before I left my job, I thought of this risk as "the one-year experiment." I learned about the concept of a one-year experiment by way of Kathrin Zenkina's podcast.[13] I could try anything for one year, right?

The risk is evolving into the reward. The big decisions and the pivot have been worth it.

23: AUDITING YOUR VALUES

I've shared several stories about my path and experiences. Now, I want to specifically talk about the tools that have helped me to see my life from a different perspective.

Are there goals, changes, or values that you're ready to start thinking more seriously about? What's truly important to you? I encourage you to sit down and really think about it. As your life has evolved, what has worked for you? What hasn't? What habits continue year after year? What have you outgrown? Are you feeling ready for a change?

I've been interested in the work of Esther and Jerry Hicks for a few years. Last year during my walks, I listened to hundreds of hours of their podcast, *Infinite Intelligence*, as a therapeutic pursuit. If you follow their teachings, you'll quickly learn about contrast: What you want. What you don't want.[14]

Have you taken the time lately to consider what you want and what you don't want? Are you wondering how to go about figuring this out? The values audit is a method that I've used more intentionally in the last couple of years as a way to do this.

I have a deck of cards that's part of *The Leadership Challenge*, a book by James Kouzes and Barry Posner.[15] My values deck has been of great use both professionally and personally. I first learned about choosing values by way of going through Kouzes and Posner's Leadership Challenge training program at my workplace many years ago, and I still find this exercise interesting, insightful, and valuable. In fact, I found it so powerful that I've even asked my boys to pull cards from the values deck and choose their top values.

On page 164, I've listed the values shared by Kouzes and Posner.

I suggest taking up to fifteen minutes to review this list and identify the five to eight values that you feel are most important to you. Yes, please choose the values that resonate most deeply with the life priorities you desire.

The first time I went through the exercise, one of the values that I chose was freedom. The concept of freedom was particularly important to me in terms of how I spent my time and made decisions. Six colleagues and I went around the table and shared our most-closely-held values. As I listened to the others speaking, I felt foolish for having chosen the value of freedom. It suddenly felt silly. I decided to ditch the freedom card and choose something else that felt true yet more *neutral* in this corporate setting.

As years went by and I continued auditing my values, I realized that freedom was in fact a top value for me. I wanted time freedom, work-from-anywhere freedom, travel freedom, decision-making freedom. At this time in my life, it was becoming even more important to me. I'd worked in the corporate world for over two decades, which was fun but not always a source of freedom.

In my life now, if I'm asked to do or participate in something, I check in with myself and see if the activity is lining up with my value of freedom.

I work from home these days, which is intentional. I like it. A client recently asked me if I'd drive the forty miles to his office to meet with a team of people. I was unable to determine how this meeting would be effective for all parties. I asked myself whether it was a good use of my time, and I concluded that the meeting didn't seem to have a significant purpose. Thus, I didn't accept the request to attend.

In the past, I would have felt obligated to meet this request, no matter what. I wouldn't want to be perceived as being difficult or even disobedient. That was my people-pleasing way of thinking, and I've been learning to retire it.

I now review each situation that arises and determine if the request aligns with my needs and values. Will it require me to fit myself into a box that I don't want to be in?

You might be thinking that life ebbs and flows and that getting things done *requires* participation in things that you don't necessarily want to do. You might believe you don't have the ability to make adjustments that suit your life. I challenge you to challenge that belief. Get in alignment with what you desire at the deepest level. Audit your values. Determine what's important and take small steps toward creating what you want.

There may be gaps between what you need and value and how you're currently living. That's normal and okay. This exercise is meant to be thought-provoking initially. Make note of any gaps, but don't judge yourself. From there, you can make decisions pointed in the direction of your desired life.

VALUES AUDIT LIST

Achievement	Freedom	Productivity
Autonomy	Friendship	Prosperity / Wealth
Beauty	Growth	
Challenge	Happiness	Quality
Communication	Harmony	Recognition
Competition	Health	Respect
Competence	Honesty	Risk Taking
Courage	Hope	Security
Creativity	Humor	Service
Curiosity	Independence	Spirituality / Faith
Decisiveness	Integrity	Simplicity
Dependability	Intelligence	Strength
Discipline	Innovation	Teamwork
Diversity	Loyalty	Tranquility
Effectiveness	Love / Affection	Trust
Empathy	Mastery	Truth
Equality	Open-mindedness	Wisdom
Family	Patience	Variety
Flexibility	Power	

Used with permission of John Wiley & Sons - Books, from The Leadership Challenge Workshop by James M. Kouzes and Barry Z. Posner, 4th Edition Values Cards, 2010; permission conveyed through Copyright Clearance Center, Inc.

24: THE POWER OF AFFIRMATIONS

A friend recently asked me which mindset tool I use the most. I responded, "Affirmations."

Affirmations are easy to incorporate into your life. You can take short affirmations with you anywhere—in the car, on a plane, on a walk, or to bed. When I wake up in the middle of the night, a short affirmation can even help me quiet my mind and get back to sleep.

I learned a lot about affirmations from the book *The Secret*, by Rhonda Byrne, and I began thinking more deeply about the concept and trying on affirmations when I was determining the next steps in my marriage.

My first affirmations were designed with the aim of improving my marriage. After that, I focused on affirmations around money. For example, "Money comes easily and frequently."[16] I would say this one over and over during my drive to work in the morning. I also tried, "Checks come in the mail."[17] I skeptically laughed at that one—who sends checks in the mail anyway? I was willing to try it, though, because I had nothing to lose. And in fact, while I experimented with this affirmation, checks *did* start coming in the mail. People even knocked on my front door to give me checks when I was running the youth tennis program.

Over the years, I've tried and used many different affirmations, especially in the time leading up to and after quitting my corporate job. These affirmations were mostly, again, related to money mindset. Sometimes sitting quietly and going over a handful of affirmations for a few minutes helped get me through a difficult day of doubting my upcoming action steps.

In A *Happy Pocket Full of Money*, David Cameron Gikandi repeats the following affirmation numerous times: "I am wealth. I am abundance. I am joy."[18] Through repetition, you begin to become more aware that it takes practice and persistence to change your thoughts. This was a top book in helping me prepare my mindset around money and abundance as I readied myself to quit my corporate job.

Having read the books of many professional-development leaders who experience tremendous growth and opportunities, I believe that affirmations can be effective and powerful for anybody, no matter the stage of your life.

Another book that I just came upon (why didn't I discover it decades ago?) is *You Can Heal Your Life*, by Louise Hay. First published in 1984, it seems to be the blueprint for many modern-day personal-development gurus. It's uncanny how strikingly similar her material is to that of modern-day teachers. Hay discusses positive affirmations throughout the book and shares stories of how they greatly contributed to her mindset strengthening and life redesign.

In the book, she also says, "It's only a thought, and a thought can be changed."[19] This book is a powerful read. I'm coming to learn more and more about the urgent importance of controlling our thoughts if we want to create positive change in our lives.

***

Full disclosure: ditching the mean voice is my biggest hill to climb.

Loops of mean thoughts are deeply programmed in my mind. They're an inner gremlin to be managed, even as I outwardly appear to be positive and upbeat.

For many years, I've understood the power and general concept of positive thinking, which I embraced more intentionally after reading *The Secret*. However, until recently, I was unaware that I could override the *entire* tape in my brain. This was a revelatory concept.

I'd always assumed that the mean, judgmental voice was a permanent fixture. I'd even thought this gremlin helped me. She was the inner motivator. If I was being "lazy," she'd have none of it. If she went quiet, who would motivate me? I wondered. Drive me? Criticize me so I'd do better? The mean voice serves a positive purpose, doesn't she? *Seriously*, doesn't she?

I have come to learn that no, a mean voice doesn't serve a positive purpose. We don't have to accept a mean inner motivator. We can replace her with a *kind* inner motivator. For example, a coach might try to motivate using fear tactics, or they might adopt a respectful, constructive tone. Why go the fear route? What's the benefit?

We can override the mean, judgmental voice, but it takes intention, dedication, and practice. We can train our minds. It can be done. I know because I've been trying it more diligently over the last year. Like, *really* practicing.

Sometimes during my day, my mind feels calm, empty, and peaceful. Then, the old, frenzied mind wants a job to do. It questions whether I should be stressing out or fretting over something. It wants to make my stomach uneasy. It wants to create a buzzy feeling in my body. My mind wants to loop and analyze a situation—potentially one that occurred years ago. My mind can go wild, even when there's nothing to solve in the present.

It takes practice to cultivate a quiet mind. And then it takes practice to accept that the quiet mind is okay. For many years, I equated quiet with lazy. Quiet is new. And it's better than okay. Reining in my mind is an ongoing process. Trust me, the mean inner voice is still alive. But she's learning that we can be kinder and still get the same results—better ones, even.

This type of thinking blends with what Louise Hay teaches, as well as with the teachings of Dr. Joe Dispenza, which I've also been studying. In *Becoming Supernatural*, Dr. Joe ties quantum physics into the concept of managing your mind.[20] I'm interested in learning more about the quantum field and experimenting with his suggested practices about rewiring old or undesired habits.

***

"All is well" is an affirmation that I learned from author and speaker Gabby Bernstein. Her "All Is Well Guided Meditation" can be found on YouTube.[21] This is an easy affirmation to use if you're busy or on the go and need to right-size your mind. I've played around with different cadences, tones, inflections, and pacing while saying it.

When I first started using this affirmation, I was in a period where all *did not* feel well. I'd repeat it and feel as if I were fooling myself. It seemed counterintuitive to practice positive affirmations when I didn't feel positive. *Shouldn't we just endure the mental punishment until we feel better?* I'd think. *What's the point of this if I'm not in the right mindset to do it?* Which is precisely the point—to create a shift in our mindset. I kept at it.

About a week and a half into practicing this affirmation more diligently, I was driving out of my neighborhood to grab lunch. I suddenly perked up in my seat, realizing, *All is well!* I felt well. Really well. I hadn't felt this way in a while. It was a sunny day, which usually gives me reason to feel optimistic, but this was different. I attributed my better feelings to practicing better-feeling thoughts.

I've also challenged myself to say "All is well" for one straight minute without getting distracted by other thoughts. At first, this was close to impossible. I've gotten myself up to one minute, but it takes focus.

Sometimes, the only affirmation you might be able to muster is "All is well." And that's good enough.

25: QUIETING THE MIND

The more I learn about meditation, the more I appreciate its benefits. The practice is intended to help humans at the subconscious level. I've dabbled in meditation for years, and I've come to identify that my inner voice tends to speak loudly over my attempts to quiet my mind. My nervous system is often in a hypervigilant state, a byproduct of growing up in my childhood home.

My inner voice likes to muse and fret over my to-do list, issues that need resolution, the past, the future, and other rabbit-hole thoughts and annoyances. Sometimes my mind will even insert a song. Recently, while I was beginning a meditation session, "The Power," by Snap!, started playing in my head. I have no idea how that high-fidelity beat infiltrated my mind. My mind is sneaky and likes its habit of looping and brooding. Soothing my nervous system is a work in progress.

Sometimes I need to listen to or ponder teachings extensively for months before I reach a more comprehensive understanding. By way of the Abraham Hicks material I'd been reading,[22] I finally came to embrace that in order to *receive*, I had to get into an open, *receiving mode*. Acutely aware of my tendency to hustle and be on constant alert, I can safely say that I don't seamlessly shift to an active (spiritual-based) receiving mode. Getting into "receiving mode" means opening up to quieting my mind and allowing ideas or nudges to unfold.

With my newfound comprehension of and interest in this approach, I knew it was time to take hold of this practice and finally release my inner chatter. It's a remarkable practice with so many potential benefits. How liberating to allow yourself to clear your mind and invite something new and fresh into your energetic field.

In January 2022, I pledged to myself that I'd meditate daily and stick with this practice no matter how it went. I'd set a timer and sit quietly for fifteen minutes. The goal was to release the thoughts from my brain. That was the goal. Not always the outcome.

Today, I'm still practicing. I don't do it daily but at least a few days per week. Sometimes it's easier to sit and meditate than others. Sometimes those fifteen minutes fly by. Other times, I grow restless and wonder how much longer I need to sit there.

Visioning is a type of meditation practice I encourage you to try, though it takes extra concentration for me. When I'm doing affirmations, my brain has something to easily articulate and focus on. With visioning, I have to activate my creativity to stay focused. Most of my visioning is around my big-picture dreams. I can play them as if they're brief movies. I have a big-picture dream about a home that I'll own in the future. I've been inside a similar home, which helps me visualize it. I put myself inside the house and take in the surroundings, colors, furnishings, decor, views, people—my personal chef is there, as is my housekeeper. I've envisioned vacations and what I'll see when I get there. At its core, visioning is about creating an energetic feeling that puts your mind and body in a place of experiencing something. This practice can help you have the feeling of realizing your dreams before they manifest into your reality.

I've gotten much better at noticing inner chatter and getting myself back to meditation or following my breath. I've found it easier to focus on an affirmation during my meditation sessions than to try to maintain an empty mind.

Some practitioners would say that a totally empty and quiet mind is the ultimate goal. Others disagree and offer alternate methodologies. I continue to strive for a meditation practice where I can sit and simply be in receiving mode—no thoughts, affirmations, or visualizations. I take it one sitting at a time. Find a way to meditate that works for you.

26: MONEY

I've mentioned money mindset several times already, as it's been a vital part of my journey and evolution. I've learned a great deal about money mindset and abundance through books and podcasts, and I wish I'd been exposed to this information and approach at a much younger age.

It's never too late to learn these concepts, though.

Your money mindset consists of your thoughts, beliefs, and perceptions about money, many of which you acquired through your upbringing. For example, if your parents clipped coupons, only purchased items that were on sale, and shopped at secondhand clothing stores, you might have learned that money is scarce and that it's necessary to be frugal. There's nothing wrong with this, but it's likely you'll chart a similar course for yourself because this feels normal to you.

Audit your beliefs around money and decide whether you want to continue holding them or whether you want to open up to other possibilities around money.

I grew up in a frugal household. My parents bought *only* what we needed. They also talked openly about how poor their families were when they were growing up. My parents were in a better place than their parents financially, but the ideas of scarcity and lack were passed on to me and normalized. The phrase "money doesn't grow on trees" was one I heard often.

As I shared earlier, one of the reasons I didn't break up with my ex in my midtwenties was that I had absolutely no idea how I'd come up with an additional six hundred dollars per month to pay his share of the rent. I couldn't fathom where more money would come from. After all, it doesn't grow on trees.

Before I quit corporate employment, one of my biggest questions and freak-outs was "How exactly will money come to me when I'm self-employed?" My logical brain wanted to know specific answers in advance. I was about to walk away from a reliable, dependable paycheck. So, what was the money plan? As an entrepreneur, a plan is prudent—but it's helpful to trust that a plan will come together. Additionally, adopting a belief that what comes our way could be bigger and better than what we could have ever expected. I charted a course for my business and had unexpected referrals and projects come my way. Just because I hadn't planned for it, didn't mean it wasn't possible. I was open to it. When they came my way, I thought "Aha, this is interesting."

What I've learned from many authors whose books I referenced earlier such as Abraham Hicks, David Cameron Gikandi, Joe Dispensa, and Amanda Frances, is a common theme about money possibility:

a money plan doesn't always have to be linear. In fact, it's better if it's not linear. Abundance can happen in unexpected ways if you're open to it. I'm constantly trying on better thoughts and affirmations around "how will it happen?" and am still trying to release my angst around that question.

I've had to open my mind to the possibility that money can flow to me from many places. Who knows where it will flow from? There could be dozens of sources—and the lottery probably isn't one of them. Additionally, the reality that I can charge more for my services than a corporate structure would allow is new yet positively evolving.

As discussed, I felt I needed to pay my dues by way of one stable job. One rung up the career ladder at a time. I had no concept of being paid for my value. Value is, of course, in the eye of the beholder. My job title dictated my pay throughout my career. The company assigned me with a monetary value based on their systemic budget rules. Sometimes I'd get bonuses based on my perceived value or contribution. It was always their program.

For much of my life, money seemed elusive, hard to get, limited. These thoughts were wired in my head, but they were just stories that I chose to believe, adopt, and hold close. I'm learning that I don't have to grind and hustle to make lots of money. Of course, action is needed. It must be smart action. What's also needed is an openness to the unexpected, to changes in perception, to the divine (hello, mindset!). Openness to both asking and receiving.

The concept that money is infinitely available seems too good to be true. That's why I'm constantly reordering my thoughts to embrace a new money mindset.

27: LESSONS IN SOLOPRENEURSHIP

In my professional career, I've worked with leaders, aspiring leaders, and teams. The topic of leadership lights me up. I love being a leader as well as being on the receiving end of thoughtful leadership.

If you take away one key point from this book, let it be this: you always have the opportunity to be a leader in your own life. Self-leadership involves self-awareness, the ability to make big decisions for yourself, and a willingness to take risks.

Quitting my corporate job in the middle of the pandemic and entering the world of self-employment required self-leadership. I had to dig deep into my motivational reserves, learn entirely new concepts, ask for help, and continue to lead my family as a parent.

Oh yes, and add to the mix writing a vulnerable book with the hope of impacting even just one person!

It was worth it.

With that in mind, in this final chapter, I'm going to share more about how I started my business.

If you've ever considered—or you've newly jumped into—the exciting world of entrepreneurship, this content is for you. I'm going to share my top lessons, learned through firsthand experience.

To clarify, my specific experience is that of a *solopreneur*. This means that I currently run my business solo. I don't have business partners or team members weighing in on my decision-making. I'll use both *solopreneur* and *entrepreneur* in this chapter. Both terms fall under the umbrella of *self-employment*.

I became an entrepreneur after abiding by corporate structures and rules for most of my career. Unlearning these rules has been one of my biggest challenges as an entrepreneur. Corporate colleagues and leaders will run your ideas up and down the flagpole. When you work for yourself, you can do anything that you want. Your work is good enough, or it's not. What you do with your work product, how you use it, how you talk about it—it's all up to you.

I was conditioned to keep pushing to make my work better and better. I appreciate striving for excellence, but it can also make you second-guess yourself. When my business was still quite new, I was writing a piece of marketing content and wanted judgmental eyes on my work, as I was used to. I sent the document to my brother, who's an excellent writer and a communications expert. He read the piece and told me that it looked great. I didn't believe him. In fact, I told him that it wasn't good and that he should mark it up. He told me that he was serious—that my work was good. And still, I sent it to someone else for proofreading. This was my corporate programming in action. My work is never good enough.

Ultimately, as entrepreneurs, we must let go of our ego and what we think people might think of us. When I have those moments where I feel I'm being judged, I'll often ask myself: *These hypothetical snarky people who are watching and judging me—are they paying my bills?* The perceived judgment of others is a limiting belief that still rears its ugly head. I have made great progress, though.

I have a friend who used to work for a major tech company. He'd tell me that his bosses would instruct him to "ship it." In other words, send out his work product. Go. Don't delay. He explained to me that products continue evolving. This made sense to me. Consider what version of the iPhone we're on right now. Suppose Apple didn't "ship it" because they wanted to keep working on it?

Sometimes when my perfectionist tendencies creep up and I'm in a loop of continuous editing, I must step back and say, "Kate, just ship it. Good enough is enough. We can tweak it later if necessary."

I follow a coach, Brooke Castillo, who tells her students to aim to produce work and put it out into the world at a B-minus level. Yes, a B-minus level. She says the fact that you're "shipping it" is good enough—because so many don't hit send, share, or post.[23] When I think about putting out B-minus work, I feel mortified. However, better done than perfect. Better to move things forward than cycle in a loop of analysis paralysis.

Entrepreneurship involves being uncomfortable with the unknown. There are no rules. As entrepreneurs and business owners, we're taking the chance that someone will find value in our product or service and want to hire us. Entrepreneurs need to experiment, try things, risk failure. It can be incredibly difficult, especially for us perfectionists. *This PDF is not quite perfect enough to hit the send button*—these types of thoughts stall our progress and prevent us from *helping more people.*

Forward movement, Kate. Momentum. That's what I tell myself.

***

Truthfully, most of the time, people won't want to hire us or come into our world. I continue to work on not taking rejection personally. I remind myself that the nos aren't personal. Of course, we can ask for the reasons behind the no—maybe something about our product or offer could use adjusting. The rejection that I typically receive isn't outright rejection. Rather, it looks more like ghosting. If I follow up a couple of times with a prospective client and receive no reply, I'll move on, though it can be disappointing, depending on the circumstances.

If someone wants to work with me, I've learned that the conversation naturally builds momentum toward how I can help, and how soon. As a service-based entrepreneur, I get to choose with whom I want to work. My options increase as my business builds. I can begin to scrutinize the best client matches for my business.

When I was starting out in my professional career and interviewing for different opportunities, I was much more flexible. Flexibility can be helpful in the early stages of a career, so you can learn what you like and don't like.

Now, I'm at a stage in my career where I know very specifically how I provide value and who my best client matches are. I've turned away assignments that don't seem as if they'll be a match or that might compromise my values in some way.

When I left my corporate job, I took time off to decompress and calm down my nervous system, only to feel my anxiety rev up when I launched my business. We all must start somewhere, and some businesses take years to find their stride, their rhythm. Finding the right approach takes trial and error.

My business was up and running less than a year after I left the corporate world. The business model that was taking shape wasn't precisely what I'd planned, but close enough. During this time, I reaudited market value and corresponding prices of my services and products and, as a result, set my prices well beyond what I was earning in the corporate world. I created business momentum. Referrals and income came my way. This certainly calmed my nervous system.

It comes down to trust. You need to trust yourself. As an entrepreneur, this is critical. Trust yourself to keep going and persevere. Trust yourself to stick to your values. Trust that results are forthcoming.

***

You don't have to do it all yourself, even as a solopreneur.

This is one of the biggest pieces of advice I can share. For example, don't delay hiring an accountant to manage your finances—the tax aspect specifically. I'd been working with the same accountant for years, but our conversations took a different turn once I was no longer a W-2 employee. I also hired a bookkeeper to monitor my monthly income and expenses. I more strictly sorted out my business finances in year two of entrepreneurship. I aligned my business checking account and credit card. In year one, I'd been commingling my personal and business accounts: not the best idea. I suggest getting your business finances highly organized in the early days of launching your business. Pay someone to help you.

My parents taught me about doing things yourself (DIY). To this day, they're still trying to DIY things that I believe they should pay someone to help them with. The DIY attitude feels prudent to me, but I'm also now wise enough to know when to delegate. Now, I'll ask myself, *Is saving a few bucks worth the headache and annoyance, given my lack of time or expertise in this particular area?* Sometimes it pays (in more ways than one) to have someone provide you with professional help.

Entrepreneurship also involves the need to embrace new business requirements. For example, I reconcile and pay my own taxes—an employer doesn't do this for me any longer. I pay large amounts on a quarterly basis. Paying taxes is a good thing: it means I'm making money. My attitude is that I'm okay with allowing large sums of money to flow to the government. This took money-mindset work. It's not easy to watch gigantic chunks of money flow out in this way, but I know that my income allows the government to fund schools, roads, and other essentials that keep communities going.

***

Another important aspect of solopreneurship (and life in general) is goal setting.

As a parent, I must concede that sometimes my goals aren't entirely my own but based on my children's needs. There are some goals that

I won't reach yet because I've committed to other priorities with them in mind. I understand how it feels to impose limitations on yourself when it comes to your goals. Maybe your goal is on hold because of a relationship, a health matter, or other reasons.

Goals don't have to be achieved in the next five minutes or five days—they can be two, five, or ten years out. I've had one goal for about twenty years, and I'll realize it one year from now. I couldn't pursue it earlier because of commitments I made to myself, in honor of my children. That doesn't mean I haven't thought about it or spent time researching certain aspects of it.

When going after your goals, you may need to tune out external noise. This means (1) not building your life based on other people's opinions, (2) taking small, actionable steps, and (3) not stopping.

The importance of not stopping, of keeping momentum going, is something I've come to understand more comprehensively through entrepreneurship. We must try things and potentially fall short. Failure can feel painful or embarrassing—but we also create our own stories and give something its meaning.

Wrangling and getting control of our mind is possible. Failures give us information. Information is positive. Information guides us. Finely tuned guidance can lead us to achieve our goals.

***

An important yet fun lesson I've learned on my journey is the one I'm going to leave you with:

As my college friends and I liked to say, "We have one life!" I've always loved that liberating statement. For me, "One life" means

"Let's try it, let's go for it, let's take a chance. Game on."

We are smart, capable, and dynamic beings on the planet. We have one trip in this body, in this human container.

Think about what you desire, and how you can set steps in motion to pursue it. Tune in to your deepest desires. Write them down. Writing them down doesn't mean you have to pursue them. But why not try them on?

Others may have opinions about your dreams. If they do, you may want to consider this: Do you want to live your life based on someone else's opinions or preconceived notions about you? How much influence do you believe others hold over you? It's a provocative question to ask yourself. Can you take your power back in some way?

I wish I'd been asked these questions earlier in my life. But I'm grateful that I'm thinking about them now. I invite you to contemplate them as well.

REFLECTIONS ON LEADERSHIP

Below are journal-writing prompts that refer to themes I've shared in Part 3. There's no need to reflect on all of them. Choose one or a few. If you find the prompts helpful, come back and answer more. Sometimes focusing on one or two ideas at a time can help build momentum. Get curious about any insights that come up, and seek professional counseling or find a coach if you need deeper support.

Suggested journal-writing prompts:

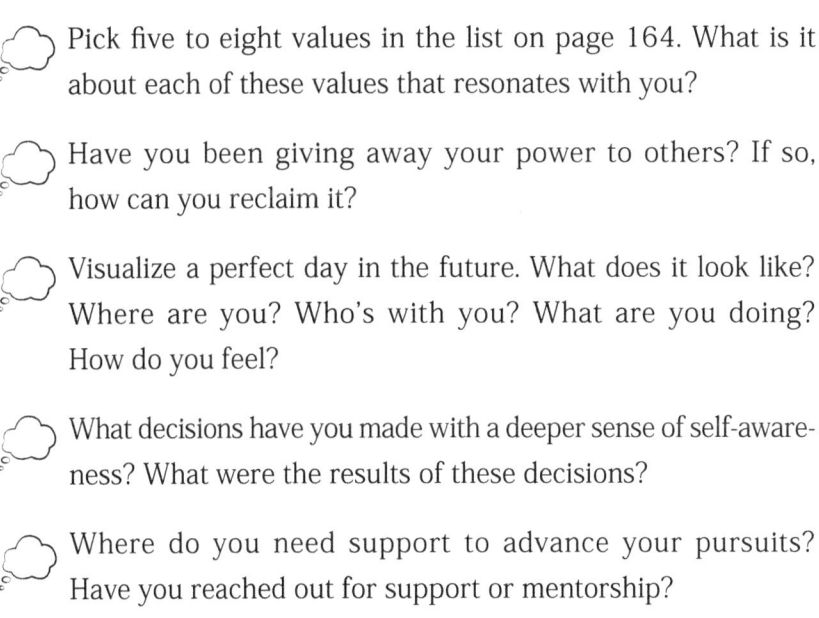

Pick five to eight values in the list on page 164. What is it about each of these values that resonates with you?

Have you been giving away your power to others? If so, how can you reclaim it?

Visualize a perfect day in the future. What does it look like? Where are you? Who's with you? What are you doing? How do you feel?

What decisions have you made with a deeper sense of self-awareness? What were the results of these decisions?

Where do you need support to advance your pursuits? Have you reached out for support or mentorship?

Here are some of my key reflections on "Leadership." I encourage you to contemplate them or consider making your own list.

Ways to reflect on money:

1. Consider how much money you want to earn before you chart a career path.

2. Audit the business structure that you're working within and figure out who's determining your worth. Get clear on your value. Then get paid for your value. This might involve working for yourself.

3. Consider the idea that the more money you make, the more good things you can do in the world.

4. Audit your money mindset. Money mindset is important, especially if you want to increase your income or wealth. You can change your mindset, starting now.

Ways to get career smart:

1. Make friends with colleagues in the human resources department. HR professionals have so much insider information that can help you.

2. Be curious, seek different perspectives, and be honest with yourself about how your work is perceived. Ask for feedback.

3. If you work for a corporation, you may not have to go up a specific ladder rung by rung to succeed. Seek information about how your company works; what are the written and unwritten rules?

4. If you're unhappy in your current role, find jobs that will provide you with better experiences. Quitting a safe corporate job isn't easy but can be worth it.

5. Do you daydream about launching your own business? Consider starting your own company. If you choose entrepreneurship, take it one step at a time. One day at a time. Keep going—momentum adds up.

Anything can be changed,
fixed, or improved. At any age.

CONCLUSION

In the final stages of editing this book, I entered yet another period of reflection.

I had to move to a new residence recently. Interestingly, I believe I manifested the move, but it's happening one year earlier than I'd expected—and wanted. So goes the Universe. Preparing for this move prompted not only physical labor, but also self-inquiry and deeper emotional reflection than I'd experienced in a while.

I might rather swim with sharks than pack and move. It's overwhelming even with movers and my kids helping. I'd thought I'd embraced minimalism in my house, but looks can be deceiving. I spent dozens of hours meticulously going through bins, boxes, shelves, drawers. I audited everything in our possession. My goal was to complete this move in record time, which would mean unexpected downsizing. Taking advice from expert home-organizer Marie Kondo, I aimed to keep only what *sparked joy*[24] for me and my family.

We made thirty or more trips to a charity drop-off center over the course of two months. Despite my wanting to sell or consign things, time was against me, and I felt a charity would benefit most from a donation. It became more and more difficult to part with so much. Still, I told myself that the time was right.

In one downsizing session, I went through photos—photos of my childhood; photos of my teenage, college, and dating years; photos of my wedding; and photos of my children. I've always loved taking photographs, and I've taken thousands over the years. I reviewed every single photo and kept the ones I deemed meaningful. I threw everything else into the recycling bin. Disposing of photos felt unsettling, but again, the time felt right.

Next, I reviewed dozens of journals, including recent ones. Reading my journals made me stop and think. My journals had a throughline of hope and ambition but also worry and fret. The worry and fret parts bothered me because they seemed habitual.

I asked myself two questions:

Do these physical books matter? It was my handwriting. My history. Did I need to preserve this history? Or was I allowing outdated stale energy and thoughts to remain in my realm?

And

Can I stop allowing worry and fret to be part of my inner dialogue?

I've been working diligently to audit my thoughts. "Energy flows where attention goes."[25] Integrating this idea is an intentional practice that should ideally be backed up with new habits. Were my journal entries old thought patterns lurking around in physical form? I had to contemplate this.

During the time when I was reviewing my journals, I was also rereading Joe Dispensa's *Supernatural*, which discusses the concept of *becoming who we want to be*.[26] Downsizing my house became a significant metaphor for lightness and opportunity. I told a friend that I was motivating myself by saying, "Out with the old and in with the new." Truly, I desired new energies.

I thought about this book. *Will the content be enough to memorialize and honor that former version of Kate?* I then considered what's next. *I'm moving. I'm streamlining. I'm headed to a new neighborhood. Who am I? Whom do I want to be?*

I can become the person I want to be. Reinvention is possible—again. And again.

As I pondered this, I collected all my journals and threw every single one of them in the trash. No sadness, no regret. A fresh canvas awaited.

I realized that today's Kate is standing on the shoulders of yesterday's Kate. She's doing well.

Who do YOU want to be? Let's get candid.

ACKNOWLEGMENTS

Thank you to the people and places that inspired and supported me along my journey.

To Rob, for sibling friendship and my big sister duties that taught me leadership. And to sis-in-law, Lisa, for her sunny, genuine self.

To Andrea, for being a best friend with sincerity and a limitless heart for all these decades.

To Mom and Dad, for being the crucial village to me and my boys, especially during challenging times.

To the incredible companies that hired me and allowed me to grow, contribute, and evolve into the business professional I am today.

To friendships, connections, and collaborators that surprise and delight me with their sincerity and effort.

To the team at YGTMedia Co. for topnotch professional guidance on my vulnerable book journey.

And most importantly, to my boys. My heart and soul. I have immense pride and joy as you launch your own new chapters.

END NOTES

[1] Oprah Winfrey, "What Oprah Knows for Sure About Getting Unstuck," https://www.oprah.com/spirit/what-oprah-knows-for-sure-about-getting-unstuck

[2] Brad Gilbert, Chapter 1 of *I've Got Your Back*, featured in *New York Times* (online), June 27, 2004, https://www.nytimes.com/2004/06/27/books/chapters/ive-got-your-back.html

[3] LePera, Nicole. 2021. *How to Do the Work: Recognize Your Patterns, Heal from Your Past, and Create Your Self*. Harper Wave.

[4] Kayla Blanton, "A New George W. Bush Documentary Explains His Decision to Quit Drinking at 40," Prevention, May 5, 2020, https://www.prevention.com/health/a32378580/why-george-w-bush-quit-drinking-alcohol

[5] Bennett, Roy T. 2021. *The Light in the Heart: Inspirational Thoughts for Living Your Best Life*. Self-published.

[6] Dr. Laura Schlessinger, *The Dr. Laura Program*, https://www.drlaura.com

[7] In particular, I've found *A Happy Pocket Full of Money*, by David Cameron Gikandi, helpful, as well as all of the Abraham Hicks material. I've also enjoyed following Amanda Frances; in addition to a podcast and videos, she has a book called *Rich as F*ck*.

[8] *The Oprah Winfrey Show*, episode 4561, aired on May 25, 2011.

9 Amanda Frances, quoting her friend Katrina, "Money While You Sleep and Other Minimum Standards for Wealth," Amanda Frances website, July 29, 2020, https://amandafrances.com/money-while-you-sleep-and-other-minimum-standards-for-wealth

10 Toni Morrison, "Does Your Face Light Up," from *The Oprah Winfrey Show*, YouTube, May 20, 2014, https://www.youtube.com/watch?v=4iIigAgDp2Q

11 Amanda Frances, Instagram post, @xoamandafrances, August 22, 2022

12 Insight of the Day, quote by John Burroughs. https://www.insightoftheday.com/motivational-quote-by-john-burroughs-12-17-2019

13 Kathrin Zenkina, "The Experiment That Blew Up My Business, Bank Account & Life in a Single Year," *The Manifestation Babe* (podcast), June 16, 2020, https://manifestationbabe.libsyn.com/website/164-the-experiment-that-blew-up-my-business-bank-account-life-in-a-single-year

14 Infinite Intelligence, Abraham Hicks podcast. https://infiniteintelligenceblog.com/abraham-hicks-infinite-intelligence-podcast/

15 Kouzes, James M. and Barry Z. Posner. 2017. *The Leadership Challenge: How to Make Extraordinary Things Happen in Organizations.* 6th ed. Jossey-Bass.

16 Byrne, Rhonda. 2006. *The Secret.* Atria Books/Beyond Words.

17 Ibid.

[18] Gikandi, David Cameron. 2011. A *Happy Pocket Full of Money: Infinite Wealth and Abundance in the Here and Now*. Reprint. Hampton Roads.

[19] Hay, Louise. 2004. *You Can Heal Your Life*. 20th Anniversary ed. Hay House.

[20] Dispenza, Joe. 2019. *Becoming Supernatural: How Common People Are Doing the Uncommon*. Hay House.

[21] Gabrielle Bernstein, "All Is Well Guided Meditation," YouTube, 2020, https://www.youtube.com/watch?v=SgjpZuGvNuA

[22] Hicks, Esther and Jerry Hicks. 2004. *Ask and It Is Given: Learning to Manifest Your Desires*. 2004.

[23] The Life Coach School Podcast. https://thelifecoachschool.com/podcast/

[24] Kondo, Marie. 2014. *The Life-Changing Magic of Tidying Up: The Japanese Art of Decluttering and Organizing*. Ten Speed Press.

[25] Tony Robbins, "Where Focus Goes, Energy Flows," *Tony Robbins* (blog), https://www.tonyrobbins.com/career-business/where-focus-goes-energy-flows/#:~:text=As%20Tony%20Robbins%20says%2C%20energy,your%20energy%2C%20amazing%20things%20happen

[26] Dispenza, Joe. 2019. *Becoming Supernatural: How Common People Are Doing the Uncommon*. Hay House.

RECOMMENDED RESOURCES

BOOKS

The Secret by Rhonda Byrne

Ask and It Is Given by Abraham Hicks

Money and the Law of Attraction by Abraham Hicks

A Happy Pocket Full of Money by David Cameron Gikandi

*Rick as F*ck* by Amanda Frances

You Can Heal Your Life by Louise Hay

Becoming Supernatural by Dr. Joe Dispenza

Breaking the Habit of Being Yourself by Dr. Joe Dispenza

How to Do the Work by Dr. Nicole LePera

The Leadership Challenge by Pouzner and Kouzes

PODCASTS

Over It and On With It – Christine Hassler

The Life Coach School Podcast – Brooke Castillo

The School of Greatness – Lewis Howes

The Chris Harder Show – Chris Harder

Infinite Intelligence – Abraham Hicks

Manifestation Babe – Kathrin Zenkina

OTHER RESOURCES

Insight Timer App

www.ingramcontent.com/pod-product-compliance
Lightning Source LLC
Chambersburg PA
CBHW051618120626
46551CB00014B/1850